Key Concepts in Starting a Business

Key Concepts in Starting a Business

Jesus C. de Sosa

iUniverse, Inc.
New York Lincoln Shanghai

Key Concepts in Starting a Business

iUniverse books may be ordered through booksellers or by contacting:

iUniverse
2021 Pine Lake Road, Suite 100
Lincoln, NE 68512
www.iuniverse.com
1-800-Authors (1-800-288-4677)

The views expressed in this work are solely those of the author and do not necessarily reflect the views of the publisher, and the publisher hereby disclaims any responsibility for them.

ISBN-13: 978-0-595-40262-5 (pbk)
ISBN-13: 978-0-595-84639-9 (ebk)
ISBN-10: 0-595-40262-3 (pbk)
ISBN-10: 0-595-84639-4 (ebk)

Printed in the United States of America

To my wife Helen, and children Jeneth, Jewel, and Jess

Contents

Preface

This book provides the key points an entrepreneur or prospective business owner must consider before starting a business. Foremost among these points is sales. No business could survive without sales.

The author developed a new approach in understanding what marketing is all about. First, he modeled it as imaging as in camera and film. Next, he related marketing to sales. It turned out that marketing must generate sales.

Next to marketing, the author deals with issues such as saving to raise capital, identifying partners, defining an effective business unit, and judging whether an idea or a product is worth pursuing or not. In addition, he unifies the effect of inflation, interest rate, and taxes. Any business is very sensitive to these factors. The author also closely examined the basis of accounting systems. Its basis is simple algebra. Debit and credit are, perhaps, the two most confusing words in accounting. To this end, the author substituted the more practical words "increase" and "decrease" to signify their meanings.

An entrepreneur will be busy establishing technical, financial, and organizational capabilities for his business. He must be super efficient to save time. Recommendations are made to minimize his time handling emails, meetings, updating websites, business security, and home bills. Long time ago, there are no emails or websites. The explosion of information in the Internet forces almost every one to manage them as efficiently as possible. These issues, if left uncontrolled, can pose significant risk in running a business. That is, the entrepreneur may find himself pinned down by these issues instead of confronting the real ones.

Chapter 1

Marketing and Sales

Marketing may be defined as the system of transmitting a business to the rest of the world. Sales, on the other hand, are the direct response of users or customers to a business. Sales need marketing, but marketing may not need sales.

Marketing is, perhaps, the most difficult aspect of starting a business. It involves money tied to the uncertainties of how well particular marketing strategies are reaching customers. A good product with no marketing cannot generate revenue. On the other hand, a bad or inferior product with extensive marketing may generate revenue. Good marketing design requires careful attention not only to customers, but also to how value and support are added to the product.

1.1 Marketing Examples

Consider the following two marketing examples. The first is the proposal for equipment, and the second is the marketing of a house for rent. These instances provide clues on the variables and mechanisms that affect successful marketing. Whether the product is a proposal or an actual physical product does not matter. What matters most is that the proposal or product is sold.

Case 1: "Selling" a proposal to management. Suppose an employee within a company writes a proposal requesting the purchase of equipment to resolve a recurring

1

issue in production, which may pose some questions or problems regarding the quality of a product.

In response to an e-mail sent to all employees, encouraging people to submit proposals to spend unused budget, one employee, after making an engineering study of the problem, submits the proposal to buy the equipment. A highly technical person, capable of answering the basic questions of the problem, is available and assists in identifying what equipment would be needed. The proposal includes complete ordering information.

The above proposal is most likely going to be ineffective in resolving the recurring production quality issue. That is, the employee has a strong interest, or zero apathy, in resolving the issue by way of the proposal. Looking at this as an example of marketing, the product is the proposal, and the customer is the management who will either approve or reject the proposal.

But for management to "buy" the proposal, he has to be persuaded of the value the proposal has to his operations. In simplest terms, the management wishes to avoid embarrassing recalls of his company's product. Hence, management must be convinced that the requested purchase of equipment will serve his interests by eliminating, or at least improving, the production quality issue.

Another variable that is important in marketing is the idea of support. A product, which in this case is the proposal, must be supportable. Fortunately, a technical person who can calibrate the equipment, write instructions on its use, and coordinate other needs with the manufacturer was available.

In summary, the proposal contains three basic elements to succeed. They are the strong interest of the employee to solve the issue, how management values the proposal, and the support for it.

Case 2: Renting a house. Consider two new homes, X and Y, that are advertised for rent. Both homes are in the same neighborhood. The prevailing rent in the neighborhood is $950 per month. The owner of X didn't spend much money to upgrade her new home. All she did was upgrade the tile and the carpet. Owner Y, however, decided to spend the time to design the interior of his home, selected granite countertops, upgraded to larger, diagonally installed tiles; and, installed the more expensive Bali blinds. Additionally, owner Y installed water-softener and reverse-osmosis systems. He also spent approximately $2,000 developing his backyard by planting several trees and installing stone pavers.

Owners X and Y both used property managers to manage the properties. The idea of using a property manager was a logical choice since property managers already have Web sites, contacts, and advertising capabilities in place. Furthermore, from their experience and credit-checking capability, they know whether a customer/renter is financially reliable or not.

As asserted before, apathy is one of the most important variables of marketing. In essence, apathy must be zero by creating a strong interest in the product. Here, two competing homeowners are vying for a rental customer. Owner X made only basic upgrades. In contrast, owner Y created a strong interest for his home by spending more money for upgrades. Later in this chapter, I will discuss a means of measuring apathy.

Owner X was asking $1,000 rent on his new home. Y, on the other hand, was initially asking for $1,250, but after about a month with no one able (or willing) to afford the $1,250, owner Y decided to lower his asking rent to $1,100. In about two weeks, home Y was rented.

In the above rental home marketing examples, Y was rented earlier than X and at a higher price. Although the price was higher, the renter saw valuable amenities such as the reverse-osmosis and water-softener systems, which provide better healthier water to his family. Additionally, the interior design of home Y provides a relaxing environment, and its landscaping, although inexpensive, was functional and pleasing. Variables such as a healthier water system, a relaxing interior, and functional but pleasing landscaping are hard to quantify or place a monetary value on. In other words, home Y offers an immeasurably larger benefit than home X.

Owner Y, after talking to some previous property owners, learned that some renters intentionally damage the property. To confront this problem, owner Y offered a $500 refund if, after the end of the lease, no damage happened to the house. This offer is an example of support owner Y is providing his renter.

Value, accurate or realistic pricing, and support are the variables that owner Y used to successfully market his rental property. Owner X, on the other hand, was not guided by those variables and as a result, suffered some losses.

1.2 Geometric Sequence and Series as First Approximation to the Solution of Marketing

Assume that you have an ideal product to sell. The product is something new, innovative, and a necessity for the average consumer. You decide to sell the product to two friends. Next, assume that each of your friends decides to sell the same product to two of their friends. The sequence of the number of products sold is 1, 2, 4, and so on. This is a geometric sequence, and the nth term is given by the formula:

$$a_n = a_0 r^{n-1}$$

where,

a_n = the nth term
a_0 = the initial term
r = the common ratio of the present to the previous term

Convince yourself that the fourth term of the sequence 1, 2, 4, ... , is 8. That is,

$$a_4 = 1(2^{4-1}) = 8$$

The sum of a geometric sequence can be predicted by using the geometric series formula:

$$S_n = \frac{a(1-r^n)}{1-r}$$

In particular, the sum of the first three terms of the geometric sequence 1, 2, 4, 8, 16, ... , is:

$$S_3 = \frac{1(1-2^3)}{1-2} = 7$$

Recall that you sold two units of your product to your two friends. Each of your friends, in return, sold two other units to their friends. Thus, the total number of units sold is given by the sum 1 + 2 + 4 = 7, which is exactly the same sum as the first three terms of the geometric sequence above.

Now, assume that the hierarchy of your friends' friends goes to eight layers. Then the number of units sold is:

$$S_8 = \frac{1(1-2^8)}{1-2} = 4,095.$$

The power of the geometric sequence and its associated series lies in its exponential growth when the common ratio is greater than one. In theory, as the number of terms increases, the sum of the terms increases exponentially. It is therefore important that the initial selling of your product be distributed as much as possible to the largest number of possible customers, even at the point of not making any profit at all, initially. The sensible strategy is to penetrate the widest possible market in the shortest possible time.

The geometric sequence above is ideal. It, however, does not happen in reality. For example, a friend may not be motivated to sell to another friend. Nevertheless, the geometric sequence defines the ideal propagation of a product to its users.

1.3 Marketing as Imaging

The geometric sequence and series approximation of marketing is inadequate in the sense that it uses pure numbers and relies on the demand of the product. It does not depend on any other variable except that the product is initially massively distributed. In real conditions, marketing must have at least three dimensions, or variables. They are apathy, valuation, and support.

These three variables may be understood better by comparing them to imaging, or using a camera. Apathy is the distance between the customer and the product. It is similar to the distance of the subject from the camera's aperture. The resultant photograph is like the product being sold, and the dimensions of the aperture, quality of the film, and appropriate lighting are similar to valuation and support. Figure 1.1 shows the relationships of the variables.

The intensity of the marketing that a customer receives regarding a product depends on how interested she is in the product, and if she has enough money to acquire the product. Additionally, the larger the valuation and support for the product, the greater the intensity. Symbolically, the intensity can be expressed as:

$$I_r = \frac{kI_0}{r^2}$$

where,

I_r = revenue per customer with apathy r,
k = a constant that depends on value and support, and
I_0 = initial expense, per customer, in the marketing of the product.

The level of apathy defines a customer's interest and financial capability to acquire a product. When a customer's level of apathy is zero, then her interest to acquire the product is very strong. Additionally, the customer has set aside the funds necessary to buy the product. A high level of apathy implies little interest in the product, or lack of the funds to acquire it.

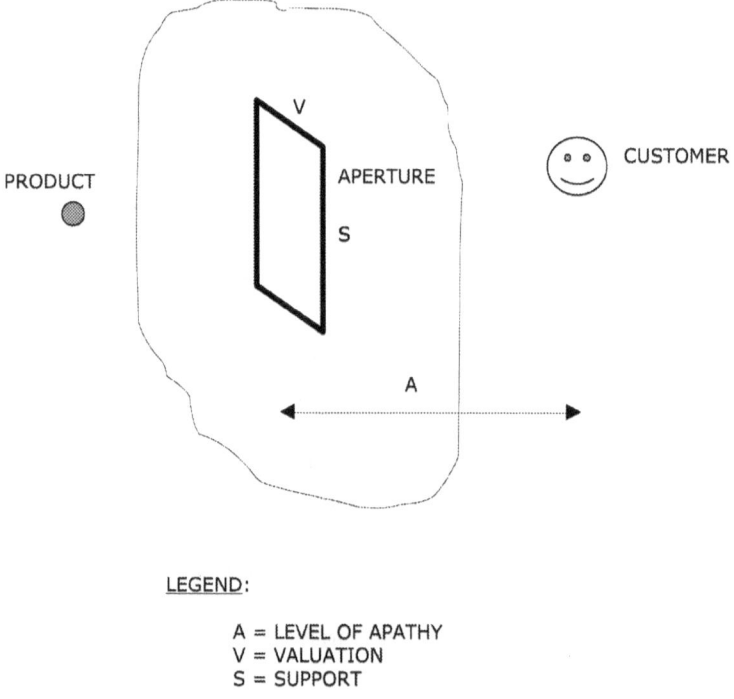

LEGEND:

A = LEVEL OF APATHY
V = VALUATION
S = SUPPORT

Figure 1.1 Marketing as Imaging

The power intensity equation also shows the very important relationship between valuation and support versus level of apathy. As much as possible, marketing must be designed so that the product's value and its support are greater than the level of apathy. The bigger the valuation and support the better. Lower apathy is also better.

Value and support, although hard to measure, can be estimated. Consider again Case 2 (renting a home) above. In the example, owner Y decided to improve his house before renting it out. Additionally, he provided an incentive to minimize or avoid damage to his house. Assume that owner Y spent a total of $10,000 for upgrades. This is the value. Assume also that he is willing to spend $500 for the incentive. This is the support. The product of the two (the constant k in the equation) is 5,000,000 (in unit of dollars squared).

Apathy level is another variable that is hard to measure. As the apathy increases, the price tends to decrease. Hence, apathy can be estimated to be a scaled version of the price (apathy, as a function of price, may be expressed as an equation of a straight line with a negative slope).

Consider again the case of owner Y in the example above. Assume that a renter is willing to pay $1,100 per month for the rent. The square of this value is 1,210,000 (in unit of dollars squared).

The ratio of the product of value and support to the square of apathy is therefore:

$$\frac{k}{r^2} = \frac{5,000,000}{1,210,000} = 4.13$$

For owner X, who may have spent $2,000 for the upgrades and offered no incentive (k = 0 x $2,000 = 0), her ratio is:

$$\frac{k}{r^2} = \frac{0}{1,210,000} = 0.$$

It is no wonder why the home of Y was rented before that of X, despite Y's higher rental price.

1.3.1 Application of Imaging onto the Design of Brochures

Valuation, support, and apathy level can also be applied in designing brochures. Oftentimes, a brochure designer confronts the problem of what to show in a brochure. Too much information makes the brochure too busy; too little makes it too brief, lacking key information. Value, support, and apathy provide the criteria for designing brochures.

Consider a simple brochure for a consulting business. With regard to apathy, a brochure should immediately attract a potential customer. In addition, the brochure must match the customer's interest. This corresponds to value. Support could be anything that comforts the customer. This may include a simple statement showing the trustworthiness of the consultant. Similarly, it may include information such as memberships to organization that establish the consultant's credibility.

1.3.2 Application of Imaging onto Web Site Development

Value, support, and apathy again play important roles in the development of a business Web site. The business should be able to communicate quickly and easily with its existing and potential customers. Similarly, customers must be able to communicate quickly and easily with the business. A Web site is an inexpensive way to obtain such a capability. A customer can easily find out the latest happenings on the business by accessing its Web site, where there should be an easy-to-find e-mail address, which can be used as a medium for communication with customers via direct response to inquiries, as well as by encouraging customers to sign up for newsletters, specials announcements, and so on.

Web site design must minimize the apathy of customers. It should be pleasant to the eye, organized, and easy to navigate. Both too much information and not enough information make a Web site annoying.

Extensive studies on Web sites show that certain design conventions are desirable. For example, Verdana font is preferable to Times New Roman. Similarly, the conventional location of the Home button is generally the upper-left corner. See Appendix B for other Web design conventions.

Design your own Web site or hire a professional. The biggest advantage of designing it yourself is controllability. After a Web site is initially published, errors will be found such as misspellings or typos. When errors occur, they must be rectified quickly because your customers will be able to see them, too. You will also need to add information and new Web pages regularly. Whether you learn to make these additions and changes, or you hire a professional to make them for you, professionalism in the content and structure of the site is very important to the reputation of your business. Web site hosts often provide software to build a Web site, or web design software is available for purchase.

If you decide to create your own Web site, spend a day or two learning the software. First, use the Help menu to find out the composition and structure of a basic Web site, or purchase a book on how to use that software. Try the examples shown in the Help files or in the book you buy. Next, concentrate on how to add and link e-mails, how to create links between your pages, and how to link to other Web sites. These are the most important add-ons. Other important add-ons include a visitor counter, a search engine function, a contact form, connection to PayPal or another payment-receiving company, and a Buy Now button.

Choose your web design software carefully, because becoming familiar with a software program takes time, and you don't want to have to start over upon discovering that the program you bought isn't going to work for you. Once learned, you can create other Web sites easily. There are reviews of web design software online and in software magazines.

Again, a Web site should maximize value and support, and minimize apathy. To match these requirements, a host should be up (working) all the time. In addition, it should have large storage capacity, a few hundred e-mails, and the capability to monitor the number of visits on the site. Avoid getting free web hosting for business. It does not look professional. In addition, a customer will be annoyed typing the usually longer web address which comes with free hosting. The benefit-to-cost ratio of paying a host is simply higher than when it is free.

1.4 Advertising Media other than the Internet

Nowadays a business owner can choose to market through several other advertising media channels, such as newspapers, magazines, radio, TV, telephone directories, trade associations and their shows; and, of course, word of mouth.

During the first six months of the business, you may spend money on advertising to show the presence of your business in the market. After six months, the money spent on advertising will stay constant because your business will have acquired a sufficient enough customer base to become self-sustaining.

There is no choice for you as the owner but to use all the advertising media you can afford. The business needs maximum exposure during the first six months. In general, the marketplace determines the price of each media. There are, however, measures that you can use to minimize your expense, such as writing to editors of news media, submitting press releases, participating in professional associations, selling by word of mouth, and developing a Web site. In other words, you have to do a lot of walking, talking, and research to enhance your marketing capability.

Recall the model of marketing as imaging. In the model, there are three variables—value, support, and apathy. Of the three, value and support should be the priority. Apathy is hard to control. It depends on the finances of the customer, which is normally unknown to you. Provide incentives such as free software, discounts, or shipping specials.

1.5 Sales

While marketing is the piping system that connects a business to its customers, the actual energy source in the business is sales. Sales create revenue. Revenue is the lifeblood of a business. Without sales, no business could survive.

The four variables that influence the sale of a product are:

1. Visibility of the product
2. Time to place the product in the market
3. Ease of transaction in customer acquiring the product
4. Indifference to the product

The first two variables are the hardest to control. Visibility depends on the relative success of marketing. Placing the product in the market in the least possible time requires effective logistics.

The third variable is the easiest to control. Once your business defines the way it will interface with its customers, then it becomes constant. Your business must be careful in defining and following sales-transactions policies—do not turn off any customer.

As far as indifference to the product is concerned, a user may be classified as strong or weak. A strong user has already made the decision to buy the product. She will try everything to acquire the product. A weak user, on the other hand, is indifferent to a product. He could use the product but can get by without it. An indifferent user may become a strong user in the future.

While the first two variables are difficult to control, your business must start marketing its product as soon as possible. Don't wait for the organization of logistics.

To this end, your business must identify all of its end users and establish communication with them.

The identity of the users must start from those with the greatest need and then go down to those with the least. This hierarchy automatically addresses the needs of the highest users first.

For a consulting organization, for example, the hierarchy may be all the relevant:

1. Governments (federal, state, county, and city)
2. Associations such as those of architects, engineers, and tradesmen
3. Industries such as power, telecommunications, defense, electronics, manufacturers, and construction
4. Companies in each industry
5. Individuals and the unorganized population

A book, however, may have a hierarchy such as the following:

1. Trade associations
2. Bookstores
3. Individuals
4. Universities

As mentioned before, your business must establish communication links with its users. The easiest way to do so is through a letter in an e-mail. Your letter must show who you are, what you do or what your product does, how you can support the potential customer, and how to contact you. An example of such a letter is shown on the next page.

Do not get discouraged if you do not get much response. Rejection is always a part of marketing.

Date

Company name
Address

Sir or Madam:

Our consulting firm, XYZ Consulting, is pleased to announce its availability to support your business. We specialize in the design of:

- Power distribution
- Grounding systems
- Heating, ventilating, and air conditioning controls
- Lighting systems
- Telecommunications systems
- Intrusion detection systems
- Fire alarm systems

Your initial consultation with us is free. During that time, we will assess the scope of your needs and provide our recommendations. Our fee is also very competitive. You may find our additional capabilities in our Web site at www.xyz.com.

Thank you for your attention.

Sincerely,

Your name

1.6 Experiments on Selling a Book

In May 2006, I experimented with selling a book I published. First, I tried to sell it to relatives. Of my two relatives, one bought the book. The other did not.

Next, I tried to sell it to friends of the family. Out of five friends, only one bought the book.

Next, I displayed the book in a retail store. The book was on display for two days. After two days, nobody bought the book. The store manager said that times are getting tough. That is, the high price of gasoline forces people to buy the necessities first. That is, instead of buying a book, people will buy gas and food first. Searching further for answers, I talked to the owner of a baby-bottle-manufacturing company. He remarked that displaying the book for two days is too short. His bottle, as it turns out, is being sold at the rate of one every two and a half months. His business survives because the bottle is being sold to hundreds of retailers in the country.

Experimenting further, I sent an e-mail to a friend showing the back cover of the book. My friend thanked me for it. It was not clear, however, if he would buy the book.

I also developed a Web site for the book. Surprisingly, in the first two weeks of the Web site, no one visited the site. Making a sale is not trivial.

First approximation to sales. The above experiments show three important variables that are important in sales—visibility, number of users, and time. As a first approximation, the sales can be expressed as:

$$S = ae^{bV_0t+cut}$$

where

S = sales
a, b, and c = constants
Vo = initial visibility
u = number of users
t = time

The constants a, b, and c must be as large as possible. The same is true for the initial visibility and the number of users. As time goes by, the number of users increases visibility.

Constants b and c are in units of cycles per unit time (or frequency). This implies that marketing campaigns must have high frequency of contacts with the customers. If your business does not market or advertise, it will simply fade away and die.

Any marketing campaign must be directed to users/customers only. It is no use to market a product to those not interested in the product. They will simply reject the product because they have no use for it. This rule applies to all potential customers, whether they are relatives or not.

Advertising, on the other hand, is directed to both users and nonusers. Advertising shows the existence of a business. A Web site, for example, is advertising. Similarly, a sign or poster is also advertising. That is, anybody can see a Web site or a poster, whether the viewer is interested in the product or not. Marketing uses advertising in pursuing or acquiring users.

Chapter 2

Savings versus Expenses

This chapter emphasizes the importance of having a large savings before starting a business. It also includes ways to raise capital. An entrepreneur may find construction skills and office skills useful in minimizing expenses. Meanwhile, the entrepreneur must continue working on his idea, even if the business has not yet been established.

2.1 Start a Business with a Large Savings

Next to marketing, capital is perhaps the next important variable when starting a business. It is from capital that all the initial expenses of the business are derived. For an individual proprietor, capital starts almost exclusively from savings.

The best time to start a business is when the proprietor is still a parent's dependent. It is rare, but not unheard of, to find a dependent mature enough to engage in some form of a self-owned business. The following paragraphs are addressed to the working man or woman who intends to own a business.

Nowadays, it is extremely difficult to save. Expenses abound, including house payments; utilities; federal, state, and local taxes; medical, auto, and real estate insurances; tuition fees, and other school expenses; and, of course, the daily food and clothing needs. You must strive to minimize expenses and maximize saving. If you are so lucky as to have a second home, you may use the equity on that home to start a business.

While it is true that relatives may contribute to some extent in providing the capital, such an approach has several disadvantages. First, there is the issue of the conflict in decision making. During the early start of the business, you must be able to make precise, wise, and sensible decisions, but you may be dissuaded by a relative who worries more about the safety of his or her contribution. Hence, there will likely be a propagation of decisions resulting in time delay and confusion.

As mentioned before, one of the ways to raise capital is to increase the rate of your saving. If you are saving $500 per year now, make it $1,000 per year. The $500 increase may or may not come from wages. It can also come from other sources.

One possible source of increased savings might be working part-time in addition to your regular work. Many families who cannot afford to buy a home use this technique. The husband or wife may work two jobs for several years until they have saved enough capital.

2.1.1 Savings from the Stock Market

Another source of additional savings is stock market investments. You may opt to invest your savings in the stock market to maximize your return. Instead of depositing your savings in a low-yielding savings account, you might purchase one or two stocks and trade them. Finding the right stock to buy—or, more precisely, knowing when to buy and when to sell—is very difficult. Most traders use technical indicators such as moving averages, stochastic signals, reading charts, and other tools to help them, but no method seems to work all the time. Be careful when investing in stocks. However, they can provide a very high return because they riskier.

2.1.2 Venture Capital

If a potential proprietor has a good idea, most often in technology or biotechnology areas, he or she may raise capital through venture capital. Venture capital provides the complete funding for highly innovative ideas. It may provide support for a proprietor's family for a year or more so that he or she can concentrate on developing the product. In return, however, the venture capital will control the business. A board of directors will be formed, who, in turn, will hire managers that could help the business. The statistics of venture capital show that only one in every 400 businesses that seek venture capital actually received it. Additionally, out of any ten funded businesses, two will succeed, two will be marginal, and the rest will fail.

In order to receive venture capital funding, you must submit a business plan to the venture capitalist. The plan serves as the blueprint of how the business will evolve over the course of five years. It addresses issues such as vision, mission, market size, competition, and intellectual properties. Appendix A shows a sample business plan.

2.1.3 Another Entrepreneur You May Know

Another source of capital may be fellow entrepreneurs whose acquaintance you may have made. Not only do other entrepreneurs have experience in raising capital, they may have contacts with millionaires who do not know what to do with their money. In addition, they may give you assistance in other areas, such as incorporating your business or forming an organization. Make sure you have your business plan during your meeting with a fellow entrepreneur. He may not completely understand your plan at the meeting, but he will inquire about its strategic details. Be ready to answer questions such as how much you will need in the first two years of your operation, how you sized up the market, and your requirements for employees.

2.2 Start a Business with the Least Expenses Possible

The higher your expenses are, the faster your savings will be depleted. It is important to preserve your savings to the maximum extent possible. Before formally starting a business, develop the skills necessary to efficiently run it without hiring other persons. Skills such as bookkeeping and accounting are two of the most important skills you will need to learn.

You may also need to develop simple construction skills such as replacing switches, installing new tiles, or fixing a leaky faucet. These skills save you the expense of hiring contractors. Hire only for those tasks that you do not want to do, do not have the time to do, or cannot do. If you have to hire, make sure that the contractor or the agent delivers. Check the better business bureau, ask for referrals, and do not commit right away. Spend another day checking and counterchecking his claims. Only commit to having the contractor do the job when you are fully satisfied.

While accounting and construction skills are required for any business, there are other ways of minimizing expenses. These ways are unique to each business.

If your business is consulting, do not rent an office immediately. It may take approximately one year before that business picks up. Instead, hire a telephone answering service, which can personally answer your customers' calls, keep records, and immediately contact you. This is cheaper than renting an office space, staying in the office for eight hours, and waiting for a call from potential customers. Spend most of your time establishing contacts with other consultants or organizations, as well as writing letters offering your product or services.

If you will be in book publishing, try to improve your writing skills. Learn how books are published. Contact a publisher and ask for their publishing requirements such as formatting, number of words, graphics, and so on. Sometimes it is amazing how the production of ordinary things we use in everyday life require such detailed attention. Each detail is a skill to master.

Minimizing product development time and organizational and logistics support. When your business begins, you will be faced with tremendous amounts of activities in the design and development of a product, marketing, defining the labor estimates and the most efficient business organization, and providing logistics support. This is true whether the capital comes from venture capital or not.

Product development takes the longest time of all these activities. Some products, such as the transistor, took tens of years before they were mass marketed. The same is true with television, the telephone, and software. These high-technology devices require proving the concept mathematically and experimentally. Simple mechanical devices, such as a can opener, are relatively easy to prove by simply using them and assessing if they work.

As mentioned in Chapter 1, marketing is so important that you must already know your market before starting the business. Get the total population of the market, sample it, and deploy an advertising campaign to sell a product like to yours. (If you are a veteran, contact the Veterans Administration to help you in marketing). Next, evaluate the results and find what does and does not work.

Repeat the above procedure until maximum revenue per unit cost is obtained. Finally, decide if there is sufficient market to make money.

If the business will create enough profits, start planning for the structure and makeup of the organization. Define the number and composition of employees that will run the operations, engineering, and finance departments. Identify outside suppliers and contractors, and generate points of contact with government agencies. Also, prepare cost estimates of direct labor, indirect labor, overhead labor, materials, and other supplies.

After defining the structure and composition of the business, start acquiring the necessary skills to efficiently run the business. This may range from learning how to use word processors to developing your own software, such as for Web sites. Expand your maintenance skills to include troubleshooting computers and application software.

It takes a long time to complete all of the above tasks. Each task, however, when completed, is money in the pocket. That is, the expense that could have been used to acquire the task is avoided. Furthermore, delays caused by an incomplete task may cause a drain in revenue when the business becomes operational. At some point, however, it may become necessary to assume a greater role in the business and let an employee or a contractor do a task.

Chapter 3

Finding Trustworthy Partners

3.1 Finding Trustworthy Contractors

Finding the right people to deal with is also important in business because not only can they cause expense, but emotional distress as well. Consider, for example, a homeowner who decides to do some simple landscaping on his backyard. He sketches his requirements for trees and pipe runs, and provides a weatherproof timer to ensure the reliability of the sprinkler system. Before giving the down payment for the work, the homeowner asks the contractor to make a sketch of the as-built condition of his work.

The contractor finishes the whole project in one weekend. However, the owner does not receive any as-built sketch and finds out that the trees are misplaced. Additionally, he sees wire running on the wall from the enclosure of the timer to the ground below. When asked if the wires are in a PVC pipe, the contractor says no.

Because there is no as-built sketch, the homeowner does not know where the pipe runs are, and he will have to dig up the soil again to find them. Alternatively, he can ask the same contractor to do additional improvements. As far as protecting the wiring is concerned, the contractor agreed to place the conductors inside a conduit. However, he refused to do the same on the wiring under the ground. For the planted trees, the homeowner negotiated to relocate them but to no avail. As a result, the homeowner was forced to plant several more trees to ensure a good balanced view of them. All of the above discrepancies resulted not only in expense, but emotional stress as well.

There are several hard lessons that can be learned from the above simple contract. They are shown below.

1. Ask a contractor to do only the work you don't like to do or are not capable of doing.
2. Don't close any transaction on the very first meeting.
3. Document all requirements.
4. Have a third party witness the formal transaction or agreement.
5. While the work is being performed, ask a third person to inspect the work.
6. Complete the payment when all requirements are satisfied.

1. <u>Contracting out only the work you can't or don't want to do</u>. Limiting the scope of work to those tasks that you do not like to do or are not capable of doing minimizes your expense and exposure to possible emotional stress. As an example, the homeowner may have decided to limit what the contractor should do on trenching and planting the trees.

2. <u>Don't close the transaction on the very first meeting</u>. Assess the contractor first before formally signing an agreement. This includes checks on his credit, referrals, and records of agencies such as the Better Business Bureau.

3. <u>Document all requirements</u>. Spend time to define details of the project. The details can sometimes determine the outcome of a project. Some contractors are not aware of the latest standards in an industry. By documenting the requirements, the homeowner saves himself lots of headaches, especially when the workmanship and method of work are noncompliant.

4. <u>Have a third party witness the transaction</u>. Once you are ready to sign an agreement, ask a friend to witness the signing of the document.

5. <u>Have an independent party monitor the progress of work</u>. An independent party can be more assertive in convincing the contractor to comply with legal requirements.

6. <u>Complete the payment only after all the requirements are satisfied</u>. Nothing is more important to a contractor than to be paid. By withholding a third or a fourth of the total payment, the contractor will be forced not only to do a better job but also to complete all the requirements.

3.2 Finding Trustworthy Employees and Employers

The above lessons apply for a one-time relationship with a contractor. That is, there is no longtime relationship between the business owner and the contractor. What if a business owner has to hire an employee, or if, in case of a venture capital investment, the entrepreneur has to report to a board of directors? Here, the relationship between an employee and a board of directors is long-term.

Whether for an employee or employer, the proposed criteria are the same. These are (1) competence, (2) integrity, (3) interest, and (4) authority. The acronym that can be used is CIIA.

<u>Competence</u>. During the start-up of a business, plenty of quick but smart decisions have to be made. These types of decisions can only come from competent people. It is better to have a few competent people than several incompetent people. The former have a clear understanding of a problem and its proposed solutions. In contrast, the latter are guided by the consensus opinion, and often base their decisions on flawed assumptions and the lack of understanding of the problem.

<u>Integrity</u>. Loosely defined, integrity pertains to lawful conduct. A business will be subjected to a vast array of laws and regulations. A business run by corrupt employees is sure to fail. The corrupt employees may succeed for some time, but ultimately, they will be caught and punished. Rules are rules. Play by the rules or vanish.

<u>Interest</u>. A person with sufficient interest in working for the business should do well. He may not be competent right away, but his enthusiasm will drive him to learn more. As he learns more, he becomes a better worker.

<u>Authority</u>. If an owner is seeking business from other businesses, he must deal only with those who have the authority to close a deal. Do not deal with middle or junior managers who are not authorized to make decisions. This saves time and expense.

3.3 Testing the Trustworthiness of a Person for Business Partnering

Perhaps the best opportunity to determine if a person can be trusted is through personal encounters. A person talks about herself in relation to her interests, opinions, knowledge, and experience. If her interests, opinions, knowledge, and experience match your business's needs, then the person can be trusted.

One of the best indicators of a person's trustworthiness is his action when compared with his word. If the two diverge, then the person is not trustworthy; if they converge, then he is trustworthy.

It bears emphasizing that finding people you can trust in business is different from finding trustworthy friends. In the former, there must be a resonance between the owner and his business partner; otherwise nothing may be accomplished. As an example, if your business is to market an impossible idea, then a person who does not believe in it may not be a good choice as a business partner. However, a friend who does not believe in it also may still be a friend. In fact, it is healthy for friends to have differing opinions because exposure to contradictory ideas may help illuminate a subject. However, a business partner must believe in the idea to support it.

3.4 How Authority may Compromise your Business

It is easier to judge a person when you give him authority. What he does with authority may determine the outcome of a business. If he abuses it, he may cause some workers to feel alienated, and as a result, demoralized. They lose their caring attitude and simply work to survive.

Abusive people are risky in business. Not only do they impede innovation, but they also circumvent business and government regulations. Ultimately, the business may find itself in court.

Before bestowing authority to a person who will run a business unit, check his or her background. If the person comes from a position of less authority, ask his or her employees for any traces of abuse he or she may have exhibited. It is possible for an incompetent person to become competent, but it is extremely difficult to find a person who will not abuse his authority again.

Chapter 4

The Business Unit

A business unit is defined as the organization that implements the business cell. The cell is the basic idea of the business. It maps inputs such as marketing, capital, and business organization to its final output, called sales.

A business organization or unit is composed of people with different skills. Some are problem solvers and some are routine workers. The goal of a business unit is to create sales.

4.1 The Business Unit

Leadership of a business mainly resides in the business leader. The leader is anyone who has the authority to run the everyday affairs of the business. He can be the chief executive officer of a large business organization or a program manager of the business's division.

The basic components of a business unit are shown on Figure 4.1. In this model, the leader issues commands and policies to guide the business in meeting production deadlines or in generating higher operating income or profit. The leader issues clear signals across the enterprise and receives feedback from other units. The feedback report determines how clear the leader's signals were. If the feedback reports show that the accomplishments of the subunits are still below the goals, then the signals may not be clear, or the other units are lacking something.

The leader usually has staff that helps him draft memorandums, policy initiatives, goal definitions, and so on. The staff consists mainly of an executive secretary and one or more personnel who excel in business communication. The filtering staff ensures that formal written policies and commands do not conflict with company policies or government laws and regulations. Thus, the filtering unit further clarifies the commands and policies of the business leader. The business leader interacts with other influences inside and outside of the business, as shown on Figure 4.2. Because of the numerous tasks and responsibilities the leader has to perform, she should be the most efficient person in the unit.

Two problem-solving units are parallel to each other after the filtering unit. These units are (1) a unit that solves low-frequency problems in the business unit, and (2) a unit that solves frequently occurring problems in the unit.

The unit that solves low-frequency problems is composed of personnel that deal with issues such a marketing, advertising, and regulations. These personnel are people with the business background such as economists, financial analysts, marketing, accountants, and lawyers. The problems they face are *across* the enterprise. Some of these problems include marketing, investor relations, and compliance with government rules and regulations.

The unit that solves high-frequency problems consists of personnel that deal with issues such as engineering, technical problems, workmanship, and parts obsolescence. Persons in this unit usually have technical backgrounds such as engineers, technicians, inspectors, and quality control specialists. High-frequency problems differ from low-frequency problems in that the high-frequency problems are usually local to the business unit, within the control of the business unit, usually temporary, and the problems may be self-inflicted due to some careless policy decisions or lack of oversight.

The business unit interacts in complex ways with outside government agencies, politicians, regulators, and perhaps financial analysts. Figure 4.3 shows the interaction of the unit with some of the most important groups or players. The most important external group to the unit, however, is the consumer group. The complex interaction between the unit and its environment requires that the unit exercise extreme care with the players in the environment.

4.2 Resonance in Business Units

Look at Figure 4.1 again. The figure shows three basic elements—the low-frequency branch, the high-frequency branch, and resistive elements. The resistive elements are staff, other employees, and all the indirect and overhead costs that consume the revenue of the business.

There is a sensitive equilibrium in the mixture of the elements. Too many resistive elements and the business cannot grow. The people in the high-frequency branch and the low-frequency branch must be interacting or else no problem could be solved by the business. Ultimately, it cannot grow, either.

When the mixtures of the people in all the branches are correct, then the business is in resonance. In a resonant condition, small power inputs to the business give a lot of power output. That is, the business becomes a self-sustaining, self-generating entity.

The interaction of all the elements in the business unit must be precise. Consider, for example, that the business finds a new market. The low-frequency branch starts looking for funds, market analysis, and break-even calculations. While the low-frequency branch is addressing the issues, the high-frequency branch must also be addressing innovations that the new market requires. Similarly, the business prepares its staff for additional employees and training to address the needs of the new market. When the time to enter the market arrives, all the elements are in place. The leader simply turns on the switch, and everything should move as smoothly as possible.

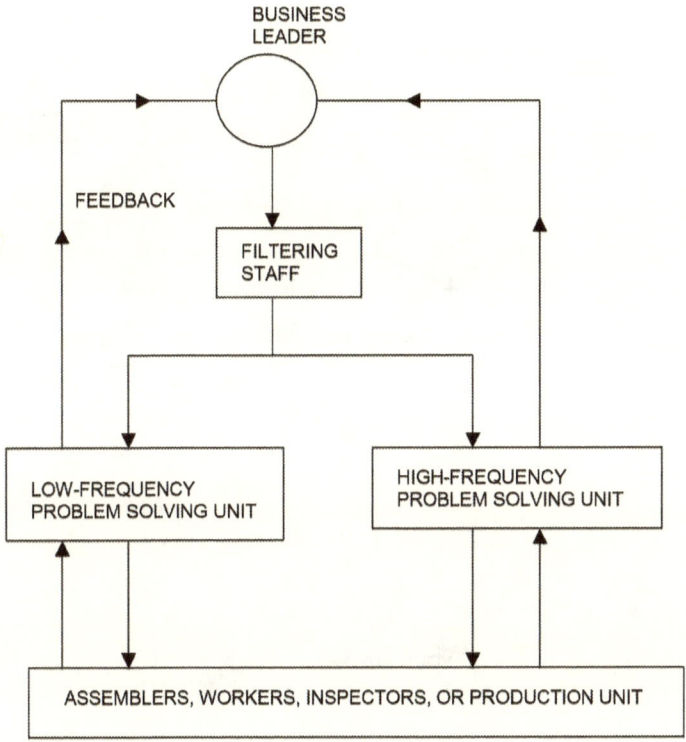

Figure 4.1 Schematic Representation of a Business Unit

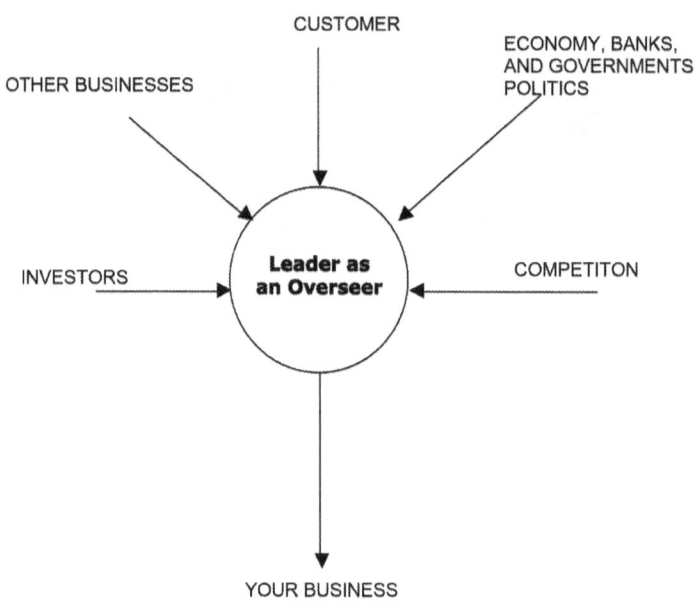

Figure 4.2 Business Leader Oversees All Influences in the Business

4.3 Measuring the Performance of the Business Unit

The capability of the business unit to deliver higher operating income and to meet deadlines has to be measured. Three approaches are possible: (1) sampling the wellness of the production unit, (2) monitoring changes in the operating income of the business unit, and (3) calculating the constants of the business unit.

4.3.1 Sampling the Wellness of the Production Unit

The production unit occupies a special place in the business unit in the sense that it is there that the actual production of a product is made. Information on how a product is produced directly affects the morale of the members of the production unit. If procured parts are always found defective, or the production procedure is found inconsistent, then the members of the unit feel uncomfortable. They sense that something is wrong, perhaps, in how the business is being run. Thus, measurement of the attitudes of the production unit should show how the business unit is performing. When this happens, the production unit starts building up resistance to the management, and information initiated by the business leader is frowned upon or perhaps disbelieved.

Statistical surveys performed once a month may be used to measure changes in the attitudes of the members of the business unit. Ideally, current attitudes should be more favorable than previous ones.

4.3.2 Monitoring Changes in the Operating Income

The operating income is what keeps the business unit operating. Budgets for daily operations of the business are derived from the operating income. Operating income should be positive all the time and, if possible, constantly increasing.

Operating income can be calculated by taking the difference of gross revenue less gross expenses. The business unit, with its financial unit, can and should measure the operating income at periodic intervals. An abrupt decrease in the operating income may signify abnormal problems that probably need the prompt attention of the business leader and the problem-solving units.

4.3.3 Calculating the Constants of the Business Unit

The business unit is composed of units that interact in a predetermined way. Low-and high-frequency problems of the unit are solved as they occur. The speed and permanence of how the problems are disposed of is a measure of the unit's operating constants.

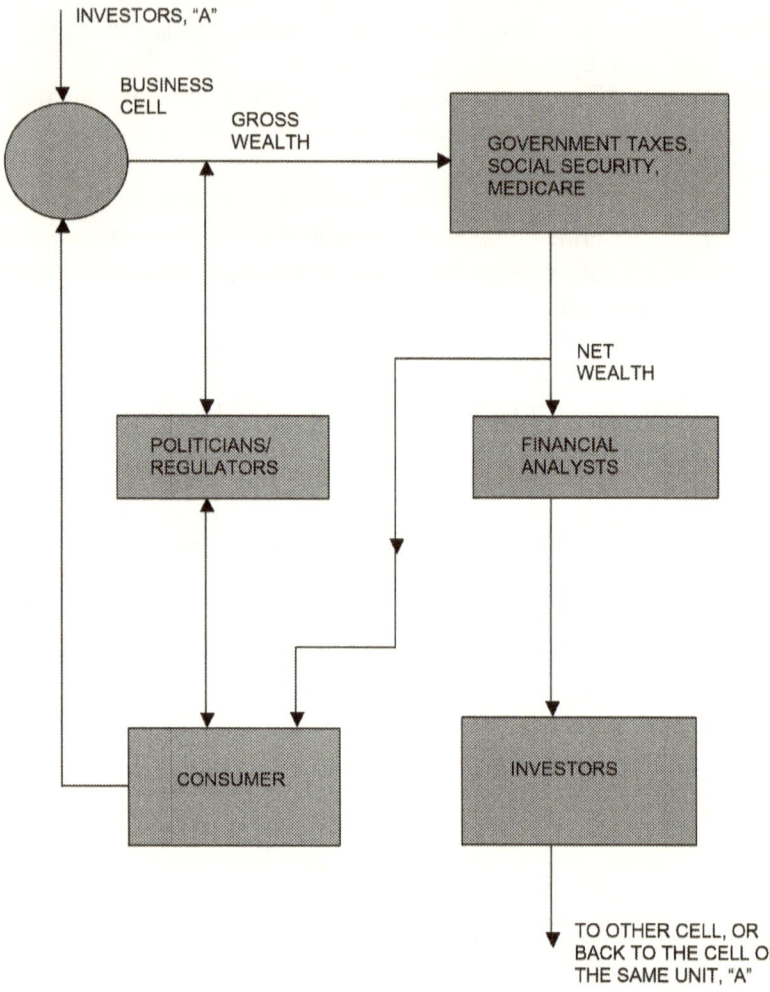

Figure 4.3 Interaction of the Business Cell with the Environment

A production unit has a set of constants for a given number of people and their skill levels in the subunits of the business unit. For example, a well-trained workforce can deliver better products in a shorter time.

The general structure of the business unit can be described as a function of a single variable that can measure, at the least, the acceleration of production. The function, in general, should have at least one zero and three poles and may be of the form:

$$f(s) = \frac{s^2 + as + b}{s^3 + ps^2 + qs + r}$$

(1)

where

f(s) = function of Laplace frequency *s*, and
a, b, p, q, and r = constants.

Applying five different frequencies and measuring the response of the unit for each frequency can measure these variables. The measurements will yield five independent simultaneous equations. From the equations, the constants can be solved. The constants represent the signature of the business unit at a given quarter, for example. They could be used in determining weaknesses in the unit.

Chapter 5

Case Studies of Possible Products

Several case studies of different ideas or products are shown in this chapter. Each idea is represented as a cell. Inputs and outputs of a cell are then defined. The primary factor in determining whether an idea is worth pursuing depends on the gross profit it can deliver and other intangible benefits. Finally, an idea is only an idea. Unless the idea is marketed, it cannot generate sales.

5.1 A High-Tech Measuring Device for Tennis Players (Case 1)

Beginning and intermediate tennis players usually have a problem with selecting a tennis racket that matches their physique, strength, and style of play. A device which samples a player's arm movement while swinging the racket can help decide if a particular racket is a good match or not. The device has a sensor and an electronic circuit, which processes the measurements and determines if the racket is a good.

5.1.1 Definition of the Cell

In this case, the problem input for the cell is selecting the right tennis racket. The output of the cell is the device. The consumer spends a long time deciding which racket is the best. The device eliminates that problem by automating the measurements and making the decision for him. The cell, then, is the capability to transform the longtime process of personal decision making into automated decision making.

5.1.2 Pricing Model

The following are the related costs for the device:

Part	Cost ($)
Transformer	1
Sensor	1
Chassis	3
Strip at racket	1
Microprocessor	100
Other circuits	50
Printed circuit board	10
Total	166

The expenses for advertising and bookkeeping will be assumed similar to that of the case for the newsletter described before. This cost is $6,520 per year. It is assumed that it will take one year to fully market the product.

The consumer in this case is a tennis store that sells rackets. There are fifty states in the United States. Assume each state has five major cities, and each city has ten stores. This gives 2,500 stores as the market. Progressive owners of stores are willing to try the device to attract more players. Some, however, see the device as a threat in making sales because a player who made the wrong personal decision to buy a racket may not come back (because the product is so accurate that it takes only one try to select). Consider that optimistically, 50% of the stores are willing to try the device. This leaves 1,250 stores. The device will be marketed for one year, and it will take $6,520 for advertising, utilities, etc. The cost from this marketing expense is $6,520/1,250 stores = $5.22/store. The total minimum expense is the sum of the basic materials expense and the last expense, or $166 + $5.22 = $171.22 per store.

In order to find out how much an owner is willing to pay for the device, an estimate of the store's net profit per year, and what percent the device can contribute to the net profit are required. Consider that a typical store has a net profit of $40,000 per year, and the device can add 0.50% to the profit. This amounts to 0.005*$40,000 = $200 as the maximum amount that an owner is willing to pay for the device.

The difference between what the consumer is willing to pay and the total expense is the gross profit. This is equal to $200.00—$171.22 = $28.78 per store. Since there are 1,250 stores, and if all of the stores will buy in the first year, the gross profit per year is $28.78/store * 1,250 stores = $35,975.00 per year. Remember that this figure is based on several important assumptions such as (1) 50% of the consumers will buy the product, (2) all of the products will be sold in a year, and (3) the store owners can increase their net profit by at least 0.5%. If one or more of these assumptions do not come true, then a loss instead of a profit may occur. Furthermore, support for the product will be required. This means that if the owner has a problem with the product, the entrepreneur might have to fix it for him. Some of the products may also fail before their warranty expires.

5.1.3 Decision

It appears that this business cell is too risky to pursue. The benefits that can be derived from it are not worth the costs. It is perhaps better to shelve the project temporarily until better prices for the basic materials occur in the future. Another alternative is to present the idea to tennis associations and manufacturers and to get a commission approximately equal to the calculated gross income above for generating the idea and designing the product.

5.2 Publishing a Book (Case 2)

Consider an engineer contemplating publishing a collection of notes derived from experiences while working. The notes are important enough that they should be disseminated to the engineering community. The engineer thinks that if the notes can be formalized into a book and disseminated to other engineers, other engineers will save time by implementing the ideas in the book.

In the present schema of publishing, the author submits his manuscript to a publisher. The publisher evaluates it and decides if the company can make a profit on it. If the publisher decides to publish the book, he assumes all the costs associated with printing, distribution, and marketing. The author, in return for his effort, receives royalties for a given number of years. The author may, if the manuscript is rejected, opt to self-publish and market the book himself.

5.2.1 Definition of the Cell

In this cell, the problem input is the savings in time that has to be realized by having a source of information that can be used in solving engineering problems. The cell output is the book that is a formal collection of the notes. The cell may then be defined as the capability of the author to compile all of the notes and rewrite them in a very clear way. Of course, the capability of the author to write also depends on how well he or she understands the concepts of engineering.

5.2.2 Pricing Model

There are fifty states in the United States Assume each state has about five major universities that offer engineering classes for which the book may be used. Each class enrolls about forty students per year. The total number of students is therefore 10,000. Government agencies and private companies may also use the book. An estimate of the engineers that may use the book is about 2,000. Thus, the consumer base is about 12,000 books. Realistically, only 50% of the consumer base may buy the book. This makes 6,000 books the realistic consumer base. The book is used every year, and therefore there is a yearly need for the book.

A publisher anticipates that the book is important enough to be published. His anticipated revenue for each book is about $30.00. Thus, the publisher can realize a gross profit of about $18,000 per year. The publisher is willing to reward the author with $2,000 per year as a form of royalty. The royalty may be good for the next ten to twenty years.

The advantage of this scheme is that the entrepreneur, or the author, need not establish a business unit. This means that the author need not be concerned about the marketing, advertising, bookkeeping, and other functions of the unit. The publisher takes care of that. The author simply writes.

Publishing a book gives the author several benefits on which it is very hard to place monetary value. Examples of these benefits are recognition in the industry, the use of the book as a ready reference in other businesses such as teaching, or consulting. Recall that much of the progress in present civilization is due to the availability of written works. Present civilization, as we know it today, may not be the same if the Egyptians had not invented papyrus. Similarly, if the Pythagorean theorem had not been recorded permanently in a written form, the world could be without 500 years of advancement in mathematics. Thus, one infinite advantage of the book is perhaps to help preserve and advance civilization.

5.2.3 Decision

Because of the tangible and intangible benefits that can be derived from writing a book, the price that the consumer is willing to pay need not be calculated. There is no need to define the business unit because the publisher is the business unit. Thus, publishing, as a business cell, is worth pursuing.

5.3 Consulting (Case 3)

Consider a longtime employee who would like to be an independent consultant. He will serve the same profession in which he served his long history of employment. Oftentimes, a company has a demand for consultants who can supplement its regular staff, especially during times of high demand. In addition, other industries such as the forensic expert industry sometimes look for consultants to serve as expert witnesses.

5.3.1 Definition of the Cell

The initial form of the consulting business is a one-person operation. In addition, it is a business-to-business unit. His initial markets consist of the industry he is employed in and the forensics industry.

5.3.2 Pricing Model

Consider that during his employment, the employee makes $110,000 per year. This amounts to about $50 per hour. A consultant may have periods with no client. In this case, he should charge at least $100 per hour to compensate for the idle periods.

Assume that the prospective consultant decides to use his home as his office. His expenses include hosting his Web site, membership to professional organizations, cost of maintaining a home office and attending luncheons during meetings of organizations. Lump together all the expenses to total $1,000 per year. With his fee of $100 per hour, it will only take ten hours to break even with all his yearly expenses. The rest will be gross revenues. Another excellent advantage of a consulting firm, unlike retail business, is it has no inventory.

During his idle time, the consultant can do other businesses such as publishing a book, teaching, starting his other line of business, or helping other companies start. These businesses are sources of incomes as well.

Nowadays, there is no stability in the job market. People are no longer treated as long-term assets. Hence, an employee could be laid off at anytime. Having a consultancy business is a helpful backup in case a layoff occurs.

5.3.3 Decision

As long as the employee is using his home as his place of business, its cost is minimal. The benefits, such as extra income, active participation in the community, potential for new businesses, and backup for income, far outweigh the cost. Hence, the pursuit of the business is recommendable.

5.4 Web Site Development (Case 4)

Nowadays it is extremely difficult for a business to survive without a Web site. A business is much more effective with a Web site than without one. As an example, consider sending a message in the form of an e-mail to a client. Whether the message is large or small, the transmission of the message is almost free. In contrast, if the entrepreneur calls his client, he pays from five to ten cents a minute.

A Web site also provides an inexpensive way to show the presence of a business in the world. By using the Internet, anybody can access the site.

5.4.1 Definition of the Cell

Define the business cell as a one-person operation for developing Web sites. The inputs to the cell are new and existing businesses that require a Web site. Output of the cell is the part-time income derived from creating Web sites for clients.

The developer of a Web site must understand not only the basics of the Internet but also sound Web site design conventions. In addition, he should know not only programming and scripting languages to enhance a site, but also how to increase its page rank and how to increase its number of visitors.

Four other important variables must be controlled by a Web site developer. They are background, color, image, and content. A Web site must have the right background, color coordination, image location, and content. Content alone could take a long time to develop. Similarly, uncoordinated colors could render a page annoying. Usually, artistic people know how to control all four variables. The average person can struggle with mastering them.

5.4.2 Pricing Model

Most Web site developers work for web hosting providers. Some developers charge from a minimum of $600 for four pages to thousands of dollars. The price is reasonable because developing even a four-page Web site could take a day or so. This does not include revisions or changes on the site. Web site hosts also charge around $5.00 per month to maintain a simple site. In all, the business owner pays a hefty sum to develop and maintain a site.

As an added support to its customers, the cell may provide free maintenance of a site. On major revisions or changes, the cell must charge its customers.

5.4.3 Decision

If that business cell has all the technical and artistic knowledge to make a solid Web site, it pays to pursue the idea. The pricing model of the business cell is competitive. In addition, the business cell has low overhead expense, making it more competitive. Hence, it is worth pursuing the idea.

5.5 The Marketing Form of an Idea

An idea is only an idea. As far as marketing, an idea is useless. There are two forms of an idea. The first is its prototyped form. In this form, the idea is still rudimentary and needs further refinement. The other form is its marketing form. When an idea is in the latter form, it can be shipped and brought to the market. An entrepreneur simply transforms the proven form of an idea into its marketing form.

Consider, for example, an idea for a strategy to win in a game of Blackjack. The idea has been proven. Assume that the developer of the idea decides to market the strategy. One way of doing it is to publish the idea. The other way is to organize a group of people, pool their money, play for the group, and charge a fee such as 5% of the capital.

Consider the first option, which requires extensive writing, finding a publisher, and selling it to the public. Further work must be done with the idea, such as proving the strategy, relating it to previous work, experimenting on other strategies, or simulation of the strategy. All the works are documented in the book. In this case, the marketing form of the idea is the book. As can be inferred, the marketing form takes more energy to realize.

Consider a more concrete idea, such as a system to quickly troubleshoot problems in electronic systems. The proven form of the idea is rudimentary. Experiments on the idea require parts that are manually fabricated. All experiments were manually done. Finally, a mathematical model proving the idea was developed.

The marketing form of the idea consists of parts that are machine produced. Additionally, the marketing form could be produced with software written specifically for this task. This will ease troubleshooting any problems. The marketing form will also require full documentation of its parts and instructions on how to assemble and the system.

Again, the previous example shows the amount of work that must be accomplished when transforming a proven form into marketing form. The extra work may take several months to years. It should not, however, discourage the entrepreneur. Immediately after proving an idea, the entrepreneur must transform it into a marketing form. He should not wait for a venture capitalist or outside financing to develop the marketing form. As much as possible, he should use his own funds to develop the marketing form. The advantages are many, such as saving the time looking for financiers and developing proposals, controlling more of the development, and owning more shares when the company goes public.

Another advantage of pursuing the marketing form yourself alone is to increase its odds of success. When two or more people interact in the pursuit of the marketing form, the probability of success decreases dramatically. Among all the people that can provide a solution, you as the innovator know more of the details, and your probability of being correct is higher than anybody else's. Of course, when the financing and marketing of your business start, you have no choice but to entertain the ideas of the financing and marketing groups. This is justified because the groups have interests in your business.

Here is the procedure to develop your idea in marketing form. First, look for the manufacturers of the parts you will need. If no parts are commercially available, develop specifications for the parts. Ask the manufacturer to make your parts. Repeat the above step for all the parts. Second, design the system according to the parts you have. Third, integrate them. Lastly, debug and, if necessary, modify the design. You may have to repeat the whole process again to refine the marketing form.

Chapter 6

Inflation, Interest Rates, and Taxes

A business constantly faces the impact of inflation, interest rate, and taxes. In general, if people have no money to spend due to higher inflation, then the business can slow down. As an example, when gasoline price increases, the money that should otherwise be spent on buying other goods is spent on gas. Interest expense on borrowed money also decreases the net income of a business. Similarly, higher taxes may reduce incomes that could have been used for investments. This chapter presents the impact of these three variables. In addition, the chapter describes the basic structure of the tax system and how tax is calculated.

6.1 The Combined Effects of Interest, Inflation, and Taxes

A business cell is very sensitive to the interest rate that the bank charges its customers, and to the inflation rate. Consider that a business unit borrowed from a bank a loan, L, in dollars. The bank charges an interest rate of b. Then the future value of L combined with the interest rate is L(1+b). Suppose that the average inflation rate is g. Then the future value due to interest rate is further increased by (1+g). Thus, the total future value (in one year and compounded annually) is:

$$FV = L(1+b)(1+g)$$

where

FV = future value in $,
L = loan amount in $,
b = bank's interest rate in decimal, and
g = inflation rate in decimal.

Simplifying the above equation gives:

$$FV = L(1+b+g+bg).$$

Thus, the L dollars was increased by (1+b+g+bg), which implies that the combined effect of interest rate and inflation rate is:

$$c_{bg} = b+g+bg$$

where

c_{bg} = the combined effect of interest rate and inflation rate

Example. In a given year, the interest rate is 8%, and the inflation rate is 3%. Find the combined effect of the interest rate and inflation rate.

Solution. Direct substitution gives c = 0.08 + 0.03 + (0.08)(0.03) = 0.1124 or 11.24%. The result shows the combined effect of interest rate and inflation rate is not a simple sum of 11.0%.

Credit card companies charge their consumers much higher interest rates (higher than the Federal funds rates). For example, if a credit card company charges 18% per year, and the inflation rate is 3 %, then the combined effect of interest rate and inflation rate is 21.54%.

Consider that an individual's federal taxable income is L dollars, and her federal tax rate is f (in decimal). Then the individual pays $(f)(L)$. This amount is deducted from the federal taxable income to get the state taxable income. Thus, the individual with a state tax rate, s, pays $[L-(f)(L)]s = (s)(L)-(f)(s)(L)$. The total federal tax and state tax the individual pays is the sum of the federal and state taxes:

$$T = fL + sL - fsL = L(f + s - fs)$$

where

T = total tax paid in $,
L = taxable income in $,
f = federal tax rate in decimal, and
s = state tax rate in decimal

The terms inside the parenthesis of the last equation show that the combined effect of the federal, and state taxes is:

$$c_{fs} = f + s - fs$$

where

c_{fs} = combined effect of the federal and state taxes in decimal.

Example. Find the combined effect of a 15% federal tax and 6% state tax.

Solution. Direct substitution gives c_{fs} = 0.15 + 0.06–(0.15)(0.06) = 0.201 or 20.1%.

6.2 Structure of the Tax System

Deductions reduce taxable income. These deductions are:

1. interest on home mortgage and second home,
2. home equity loan,
3. real estate tax,
4. vehicle license fees,
5. legal and accounting fees,
6. hobby not to exceed 2% of AGI,
7. contribution to an IRA account,
8. employee business expense (use Form 2106), and
9. Coverdell Education Savings Account (education IRA).

Tax is increased by other incomes. These other incomes include all the interest and ordinary dividends, and cancellation of debt (use Form 1099-C).

If an individual is self-employed, the following, in addition to the above, are deductible and decreases the taxable income:

1.   contribution to retirement,
2.   premium on health insurance,
3.   moving expenses, and
4.   one-half of self-employment income

6.3 Tax Calculations

The calculations for tax involve five quantities. These are adjusted gross income, taxable income, the tax as a percent of the taxable income, the net tax which is the percent of the taxable income less credits, and the actual tax, which is the net tax plus the other taxes.

Adjusted Gross Income. The adjusted gross income is the total income reduced by all possible deductible incomes. It is shown below:

> ADJUSTED GROSS INCOME (also called AGI on IRS form line 33 or 34) = Wages + other incomes - (IRA + student loan interest + medical savings account [MSA] + moving expenses).

Reducing wages and increasing IRA contributions and other items inside the parentheses will reduce the adjusted gross income.

Taxable Income. The taxable income is simply the difference between the adjusted gross income and the sum of all itemized deductions and allowances for exemptions. Its formula is shown below:

> TAXABLE INCOME (IRS form line 39) = Adjusted Gross Income - (Itemized Deductions + Exemptions).

Increased itemized deductions decrease the taxable income.

Tax. Tax laws change every year. Sometimes the tax bracket, in percent, will increase or decrease in a year. It all depends on the laws enacted by Congress. Once the taxable income is known, the amount is multiplied by a certain percent. This is the tax and is shown on line 42:

TAX (line 42) = taxable income times k, where k = is the corresponding percent of the taxable income.

Net Tax. The tax is further decreased by credits such as foreign tax credit, dependent care expenses, and others. Line 51 shows the net tax:

NET TAX (line 51) = Tax (line 42) - (foreign tax credit + credit for child and dependent care expenses + education credits + child tax credits + adoption credit).

A credit directly reduces the tax by 100% of the credit amount. Deduction, on the other hand, decreases the tax in proportion to the tax bracket in percent and the deductible amount.

Consider a deduction of $100 and a tax bracket of 20%. The deduction saves the taxpayer $20. On the other hand, if the deduction is treated as a credit, it saves the taxpayer $100.

Actual Total Tax. The actual total tax is the sum of the tax plus the other taxes and is shown below:

ACTUAL TOTAL TAX (IRS form line 57) = Net Tax (line 51) + Other Taxes.

While a credit directly decreases tax, other tax directly increases it. Other taxes include tax owed, such as self-employment tax, tax on an IRA and other retirement plans, and household employment tax. Note that the tax on an IRA has to be treated carefully. If one withdraws money from an IRA account that is losing money, that loss should be considered as the basis in computing the penalty for early withdrawal.

Summary. The above elements of determining a tax can be conveniently represented by the equation:

$$t = (a - d)k - c + q$$

where

t = actual total tax,
a = adjusted gross income,

d = sum of all deductions,
k = tax bracket in decimal,
c = sum of all credits, and
q = other taxes.

Simplifying the equation gives:

$$t = ak - dk - c + q \,.$$

Examine the terms dk and c in the last equation. A deductible, d, and tax bracket, k, reduce the tax by dk. If the same deductible, d, is treated as a credit, c, then the tax is reduced by exactly d (as opposed to dk in the first case).

Chapter 7

Accounting Systems

Accounting is the recording of all transactions and classifying each transaction into assets, liabilities, or owner's equity. It shows the financial condition of a business at any time. This chapter discusses the two basic types of accounting systems and how entries are made in accounts. In addition, it shows how balance sheets and income statements are prepared. Because *debit* and *credit* are two terms that can confuse a business owner the terms *increase* and *decrease* will be discussed to aid understanding. A business's relative performance may be found using indicators of business performance.

7.1 The Cash versus the Accrual Accounting Systems

Accounting is used to record and ultimately measure how business inputs in terms of resources are transformed into outputs of incomes. The single most important objective of any business is to increase income. With higher net income, the business can afford to pay its interest expenses and pay dividends to its owners.

Two accounting systems are used. They are the cash accounting system and the accrual accounting system. In cash accounting, a firm simply subtracts all the disbursements, or payments, from all the cash receipts to get the net operating cash flow. The system, however, is flawed because of the time value of money. A firm, for example, may decide to buy equipment in its first year of operation.

The cost of the equipment, and its depreciation, should be distributed along the equipment's economic life. Additionally, a firm may buy some of its supplies using credit. The ensuing debt belongs to accounts payable. Because accounts payable is not cash, the firm could not subtract such a disbursement using the cash accounting system.

The accrual accounting system is better for recording this type of debt than the cash accounting system because it can represent the cost and depreciation of equipment, as incremental values, in its economic life. Furthermore, the system can accommodate changes in the firm's accounts payable and accounts receivable.

7.2 The Importance of the Period in which a Product or Service is Rendered

Financial statements are usually prepared monthly, quarterly, and annually. The quarterly statement is derived from the monthly statements. The annual statement is derived from the quarterly statements. The basic accounting period is therefore monthly. During the month, the business derives revenues or inflows, and pays expenses or outflows.

Consider that during the month M, a firm produces a product or a service. In this month, P expense outflows were incurred, and Q revenue inflows were received. The accrual accounting system requires that the P outflows and Q inflows should be recorded only for the month M. Some exceptions apply. They are:

1. revenue inflow from the next month, N, is allowed provided that the production of the product or the rendering of the service occurred in the present month, M, and

2. expense outflow for the next month, N, may be paid in the present month, M.

Note that the above rules require that revenues from the previous month could not be added to the revenue to the present month. The rules are based on:

1. the realization principle, which states that the revenue realized during this period came from cash or claims to cash when the product or services are made during the period, and

2. the matching principle, which states that the expenses incurred to produce and sell a product or service should occur during the revenue period.

7.3 Relationship of the Basic Expense Accounts

The basic expense accounts of most businesses include the following:

1. equipment,
2. rent,
3. supplies,
4. salaries and wages,
5. material for the product,
6. interest on loan,
7. taxes, and
8. utilities.

Distinction should be made between cash disbursements and expense for each account. The cash disbursement for an account is the actual cash paid for the account independent of the accounting period. The expense paid for the account is the "distributed" payment for the accounting period. The accounting period is the period in which the goods or services are produced. For example, a firm may have paid $600,000 for equipment with ten years of economic life. The cash disbursed for the equipment account is $600,000, but the expense for the accounting month is $600,000 divided by 120 months, or $5,000.

In general, the following three relationships exist between cash disbursements and expense for the basic accounts:

1. the cash disbursements for equipment, rent, and supplies are greater than the expense,
2. the cash disbursements for salaries and wages, basic material, interest on loans, and taxes are less than the expense, and
3. for utilities, the cash disbursements and expense are equal.

As an example, Table 7.1 shows the above important relationships.

Table 7.1 Example of Cash Disbursement and Expense

Nature of the Sacrifice	Cash Disbursed in February in $	Expense Recognized in February in $
Equipment (See Note 1)	600,000	10,000
Rent (See Note 1)	60,000	20,000
Supplies (See Note 1)	20,000	15,000
Salaries and wages (See Note 2)	120,000	150,000
Basic material (See Note 2)	130,000	145,000
Interest on loans (See Note 2)	0	6,000
Federal income tax (See Note 2)	0	24,000
Utilities (See Note 3)	10,000	10,000
Total	940,000	380,000

Note 1: These accounts show cash disbursements > expenses for the same month.
Note 2: These accounts show cash disbursements < expenses for the same month.
Note 3: These accounts show cash disbursements = expenses for the same month.

7.4 Distinction between Income, Income from Continuing Operations, and Net Income

Income is the wealth, or the difference between the total revenue and the total expense. The total revenue and total expense are directly related to the production of a product or service. This relationship is shown below:

Income = Revenue – Total Expense.

Income from continuing operations, however, is the sum of the income and gain (or loss) not routinely related in the production of the product or service. An example of such a gain is the sale of equipment. Specifically income from continuing operations can be:

income from continuing operations = Income + gain, or
income from continuing operations = Income – loss.

There is a class of unusual gains and losses (such as tornado damage or earthquake damage) which infrequently happen to a business. Such gains or losses are called extraordinary gains or losses. The net income is obtained by directly subtracting or adding ordinary gain or loss, respectively, from income from continuing operations. That is,

net income = income from continuing operations + extraordinary gain, or
net income = income from continuing operations – extraordinary loss.

7.5 The Balance Sheet

The balance sheet gives information on the money and resources the management used and accounts that directly affect net income. The accounts can be classified into assets, liabilities, or owner's equity. Table 7.2 is an example of a balance sheet.

Assets are resources that are owned by a business. Assets contribute to future profitability of the business. Examples of assets are cash on hand, accounts receivable, patents, land, buildings, and equipment. The assets are used to produce a product that will earn net income.

Liabilities are future sacrifices of economic benefits to obtain assets. They are debts to purchase assets. Liabilities include accounts payable, wages and salaries, and mortgages on land and buildings.

Owner's equity represents the interest in the assets after deducting liabilities. It is the residual, or remaining, asset after liabilities are paid. The beginning owner's equity, when the expense is zero, is called paid-in capital. Retained earnings, on the other hand, is the cumulative excess of (1) net income over net losses, and (2) dividend distributions or withdrawals by owners. The two accounts fall under owner's equity.

7.5.1 The Balance Sheet Equation

The balance sheet equation is given as:

Assets = Liabilities + Owner's Equity.

Under ideal conditions, at any time, the two sides of the equation should be equal. Solving for liabilities in the equation gives:

Liabilities = Assets – Owner's equity.

If the equality symbol is replaced by the greater than inequality symbol, then:

Liabilities > Assets – Owner's Equity.

The inequality means that the business is in the state of bankruptcy. This is similar to a household that has accumulated large credit card debts, and can no longer pay the principal and interest on its loans. It means that it has insufficient funds to pay for the difference between assets and owner's equity. If liabilities increase faster than the difference between assets and owner's equity, then a company is not generating enough net income. The condition becomes dangerous when operations to produce products or services generate loss instead of income.

Complete stability in the financial condition of a company occurs when the company has no liability. This means that

Assets = Owner's Equity. (condition of complete stability)

Under this condition, no bank can force the company into bankruptcy, even if the company is losing from operations.

7.5.2 Making Entries on the Balance Sheet

Entries in a balance sheet are based on the principle that the cost of a resource is its price. Thus, entries on the balance sheet are prices paid. Accounts used in income statements are the same accounts used in the balance sheet. In a balance sheet statement, however, the accounts are further grouped into assets, liabilities, and owner's equity. A basic balance sheet has the following basic accounts:

1. assets consisting of cash, accounts receivable, prepaid rent, inventory of the basic material, supplies, equipment, and accumulated depreciation,
2. liabilities consisting of accounts payable, accrued liabilities, and bank loan payments, and
3. owner's equity consisting of paid-in capital and retained earnings

Cash consists of the paid-in capital and investments to acquire capital assets such as equipment. Accounts receivable represents the amount customers owe to the business. Conversely, accounts payable represents the amount the business owes to its suppliers.

Table 7.2 An Example of a Balance Sheet

ASSETS = LIABILITIES + OWNER'S EQUITY

Event	Cash	A/R	Prepaid Rent	Basic Material	Supplies	Equipment	Depreciation	A/P	Paid-in Capital	Retained Earnings
Initial position	$750								$750	
Purchase equip-ment	(600)					$600				
Prepay rent	(60)		$60							
Purchase supplies	(20)				$20					

Note: A/R means Accounts Receivable (money coming in)
A/P means Accounts Payable (money going out)

Three stages are used to completely prepare a balance sheet. In each stage there are entries called events. These stages are external transactions, income measurements, and internal adjustments.

External transaction. External transactions are business exchanges between the firm and other external businesses such as suppliers, banks, and owners. Events in external transactions occur before sales. External transactions represent the operations of the business in producing and selling a product or service. Entries in external transactions are cash disbursements and *not* expenses.

Income measurements. Income measurements include entries in the balance sheet to allocate revenues and expenses to their appropriate accounts. These events are entries from sales to payments of salaries and wages. Entries in income measurements are expenses.

Internal adjustments. Events or entries during internal adjustments are shown from cost of basic material to payment of dividends. An internal adjustment event recognizes expense after or subsequent to when a resource was acquired from an external transaction. Internal adjustments include expense for depreciation, and ordinary gains or losses.

7.5.3 Some Rules to Follow When Making Accounting Entries

Entries in a balance sheet always come in pairs. Some entries are both positive (represented by "+" in the following rules), some are both negative (represented by "()"), or one of the pair is positive and the other is negative. The following are intended as rules when making entries. The rules are based on (1) satisfying the equality in the balance sheet equation, and (2) providing "rules of thumb" on how entries in the balance sheet are made.

Rules to maintain the equality of the balance sheet equation:

- Entries on the *same* side of the balance sheet equation will have *both* + and ().
- Entries on both sides of the equation will have *either* () only, or + only, but *not both*.

Rule for the external transaction stage:

- Most of the cash disbursements in external transactions involve the *assets side* only, and if the liabilities side is required, the entry is usually made on the accounts payable side only. The cash account in the asset side is usually decreased as indicated by ().

Rules for income measurements:

- Almost all entries in the income measurement stage involve entries on retained earnings.

- Expense entries in the income measurement stage are *calculated using the data from the external transactions.*

Rules for internal adjustments:

- Internal adjustments are made on *prepaid rent, inventory, accounts payable, supplies, depreciation, cash (for dividends), and retained earnings.*
- Dividends are *not included in the income statement* but are included in the balance sheet. Dividend payment is usually shown near the end of the balance sheet.
- The "formal" income statement can be derived from the income measurement stage of the balance sheet provided care is exercised to include the actual expenses during the period. For example, the salaries and wages account requires the addition of the cash disbursement and recognition of salaries and wages as actual expense. This follows from the relationship between cash disbursements and expense. In particular, the cash disbursements for salaries and wages are less than the expense.

7.6 The Cash Flow Statement

The cash flow statement shows how cash is generated from the various accounts of the balance sheet. The cash flow statement is important because it shows the accounts that are profitably weak The business's actual cash is used to pay interest and short-term liabilities.

Cash flow can be classified according to the type of its source. An operating cash flow is one that comes from the operations of the business. Cash flow from investing is derived from non-cash assets such as buildings, equipment, land, and so on. Selling equipment, for example, can generate cash to the business. Cash flow from financing arises from the increase in the liabilities or owner's equity. A business may borrow money from a creditor to increase its cash flow. Similarly, the business may sell shares of its own stock to raise more capital.

A company usually goes bankrupt when it does not have enough cash to pay its creditors. The absence of enough cash can result from various reasons. The chief reason is the diminishing demand for its products or services. First, the net income of the business goes down until it becomes a loss. Next, creditors will demand payments for interest in their capital. If the business does not have the cash right away, it may have to sell some of its assets or lay off some of its employees. If its market continues to deteriorate, the creditor may force the business into bankruptcy.

7.6.1 Cash Flow from the Cash Account of the Balance Sheet

The cash flow from the cash account can be found by taking the difference between the cash of the present period and the previous period. If the difference is positive, then the cash flow is positive. Conversely, if the difference is negative, then the cash flow is negative.

7.6.2 Steps in Preparing the Cash Flow Statement from Non-cash Accounts of the Balance Sheet

Two basic steps are required to completely determine the cash flow of a business. They are (1) analysis of the balance sheet statement to classify accounts according to type of source for cash flow and finding the amount that the cash changed, (2) analyzing cash flow from investing, financing, and operations activities, and (3) preparing the cash flow statement.

The first step in the analysis of cash flow is finding the change (increase or decrease) of all non-cash accounts in the balance sheet. The change is the difference in amounts between the ending period and beginning period. If the change is a positive number, then it is an increase; otherwise, it is a decrease. Next, each of the accounts, from the point of view of cash flow, can be investing, financing, or operations.

The second step in cash flow analysis is shown by the following paragraphs.

Cash flow from investing. The balance sheet is inspected to find out if old equipment is sold, and/or new equipment bought. The depreciation of the sold equipment is part of the cash flow from investing, but the depreciation of the new equipment is part of cash flow from operations. The disposed value of the sold equipment less its depreciation is the source of cash.

Cash flow from operating activities. To find the cash flow from operating activities, four sub-activities are analyzed. These sub-activities are (1) cash receipts from customers, (2) cash payments for merchandise, (3) cash payments for operating expense, and (4) equipment depreciation. The cash receipts from customers, cash payments for merchandise, and cash payments for operating expense are shown below:

1. cash receipts from customers = revenue–change in the accounts receivable,

2. cash payments for merchandise = cost of sales + change in inventory – change in accounts payable, and

3. cash payments for operating expense = operating expenses + increase in prepaid expenses – increase in accrued liabilities.

Note that equipment depreciation does not require cash, so no equation is provided.

In the above equations the "change" increases, but if the change decreases, then the arithmetic operations x + y and x–y become x–y and x + y, respectively. This may be cumbersome. The following representation of the above equations may be easier:

1. cash receipts from customers = revenue + (increase in the accounts receivable),

2. cash payments for merchandise = cost of sales + increase in inventory + (increase in accounts payable), and

3. cash payments for operating expense = operating expenses + increase in prepaid expenses + (increase in accrued liabilities).

In the latter representation, the parenthesis pair "()", means the negative of the number or account. Thus x + (y) actually means x–y. Another way of looking at the symbol "()" is to treat it like a mathematical operator. If z is a quantity, then (z) is its opposite, and ((z)) = z. Thus, in equation one above, if the "increase in the accounts receivable" becomes "decrease in accounts receivable" (after the calculation of the increase or decrease according to step number one above) then equation one becomes:

cash receipts from customers = revenue + ((decrease in the accounts receivable)), or

cash receipts from customers = revenue + decrease in the accounts receivable.

Similarly, if the "increase in inventory" from equation two is actually "decrease in inventory" then equation two becomes:

cash payments for merchandise = cost of sales + (decrease in inventory) + (increase in accounts payable).

The quantity "(decrease in inventory)" means that it has to be subtracted from the cost of sales.

Notice that in the above equation, the terms with keywords "accounts" and "accrued" are in parentheses. This observation should help remember the equations.

The last step in cash flow analysis is the preparation of the cash flow statement. It is basically a summary of the three sections: cash flow from operating activities, cash flow from investing activities, and cash flow from financing activities. The net result is also shown at the bottom of the statement.

7.6.3 Interpreting the Cash Flow Statement

The general method of interpreting the results of the cash flow statement involves a two-step procedure. The first step is to identify the entries in the statement with parentheses because each entry decreases the overall cash flow. The next step is to find the cause of the parenthetical entries. For example, if the accounts receivable has parentheses, then the account has increased, which implies that the collections department may not be efficient in collecting payments from customers.

7.7 Indicators of Business Performance

Conventional indicators of business performance use net income, assets, owner's equity, and other accounts such as revenue, dividends, and total shares outstanding. In the following indicators, "average" means the mean of the beginning and the end of a period. The following indicators can be used to estimate the performance of a business:

1. earnings per share = net income/total shares outstanding (including the stock options, use the fully diluted earnings per share if available),
2. earnings yield = (EPS–dividend)/(lowest stock price in the year + highest stock price in the year)/2,
3. return on assets = (net income + interest expense)/average total assets,
4. return on owner's equity = net income/average owner's equity,
5. net income to sales = net income/sales (revenues), and
6. return on owner's equity = net income/average owner's equity.

The following are the indicators of risk in the business:

1. current ratio = current assets/current liabilities,
2. acid-test ratio = quick assets/current liabilities,
3. debt to assets ratio = total liabilities/total assets, and
4. times interest earned = (income before tax + interest expense)/interest expense.

Note that none of the indicators employ cash flow as a variable in any of the indicators. Yet, the cash flow is so important that somehow it has to be used. The following indicator may be used to measure the efficiency of the business:

business efficiency = net increase in cash flow/net income.

Recall that one of the important functions of the cash flow statement is the identification of accounts that are causing decreases in cash flow. The above indicator is justified because as the cash flow increases, the efficiency of the business also increases.

7.8 Double Entry Using Credit and Debit

The accrual system of accounting is a double-entry system. The entries can be both inflows, both outflows, or one inflow and one outflow. Consider the balance sheet equation:

$A = L + C$

where

A = assets,
L = liabilities, and
C = capital.

If an inflow, X, is added to A, then the same inflow, X, should be added to L + C. Thus:

$$A + X = L + C + X$$

If outflow, Y, is subtracted from A, then the same outflow, Y, should be subtracted from L + C. The result is:

$$A - Y = L + C - Y$$

The last two equations state that an increase in one side of the equation requires the same increase on the other side. Similarly, a decrease in one side requires the same decrease on the other side.

Consider next that only one side of the balance sheet equation is to be used. To maintain the equality, an inflow on the side should have the same outflow on the *same* side. For example, consider that an amount, Z, has to be entered on the asset side, A, of the balance sheet equation. Then to maintain the equality of the balance sheet:

$$A + Z - Z = L + C$$

Similarly, if the amount, Z, is to be entered on the liability and capital side only, then:

$$A = L + C + Z - Z$$

The last two equations are very important (although they are not formally presented in accounting books). The last two equations show that the sum of the two entries on the *same* side is zero. Thus, if the amount increases an account, then the same amount should decrease another account (both accounts on the same side of the equation).

Using the words *increase* and *decrease* can determine all of the requirements of an accrual accounting system. The industry, however, employs the words *credit* and *debit*. Furthermore, the industry uses the parenthesis pair "()" to indicate a decrease in an account. The two important rules have to be remembered:

- an increase in any account on the liability or owner's equity side is a *credit*, and
- an increase in any account on the asset side is a *debit*.

The opposite is true for a decrease in an account. That is:

- a decrease in any account on the liability or owner's equity side is a *debit*, and
- a decrease in any asset account on the asset side is a *credit*.

The above rules can be remembered by starting from the owner's equity. Since an increase in the owner's equity is good, then it (the increase in equity) must be a *credit*. The increase in the asset must therefore be a *debit*. Tables 7.3 and 7.4 further amplify the subtle points described above.

Table 7.3 The Use of Credit and Debit With an Entry to Both Sides of the Balance Sheet Equation

ENTRIES ON *BOTH* SIDES OF THE EQUATION

Asset	Liabilities Or Owner's Equity
increase debit	increase credit
decrease (credit)	decrease (debit)

Table 7.4. The Use of Credit and Debit When Entries are on the Asset Side Only

ENTRIES ON THE *ASSET* SIDE ONLY

Account 1 on the Asset Side	Account 2 on the Asset Side
increase debit	decrease (credit)
decrease (credit)	increase debit

In the above tables, the parentheses "()" indicates the decrease in the account.

Chapter 8

Time Management

Immediately after starting a business, the entrepreneur will find herself pressed for time. It is common for her to work twelve hours a day. Most of the activities she will be working on involve organizing her business. This includes keeping track of receipts, establishing contacts, attending trade shows, going on meetings with trade associations, developing Web sites, following up on leads, and so on.

8.1 Accounting Software and Receipts

Early on in the business, learn as much as possible about the accounting software you will use. Spend at least a day or two navigating its menus. Ensure that data generated by the software can be downloaded to tax software.

The ideal tax accounting software is one that allows you to enter data in a tabulated format or journal. Data for accounts, assets, liabilities, and capital should be automatically extracted from the journal. In addition, the software should automatically determine cost of operations, gross profit, net profit, and other figures of interest.

Get a shoe box or a plastic box to store all your receipts. Label each receipt according to the index in your journal. This way, you can easily sort the receipts if there is an audit in your business.

8.2 Establishing Contacts

Marketing connects your business to your customers. Start compiling a list of contacts you meet at trade shows, meetings, or informal parties. Use Excel to generate the list. The list should include the usual telephone numbers, addresses, business names, domain names, and e-mail addresses. Secure the privacy of your list by storing it in a computer that is not connected to the Internet.

Once you have made contact with a person, send him a note the following day or two. This reinforces your relationship with him. There is nothing more important to a potential customer than for you to remember his name and business. By showing your interest with the person and his business, you are marketing your business. Use e-mail as much as possible. An e-mail shows your domain name. This way, he will have a permanent record of your business in addition to your domain name.

Send another e-mail to your contacts whenever a new event happens in your business, such as an innovation or capability you have developed or a new product you have just completed. On major holidays, such as Christmas, send another e-mail.

8.3 Paying Bills Online and Use of a Credit Card Specifically for Business

While paying bills online may present privacy issues, it pays to use that service for paying home bills. Remember, you will be busy. It saves you time by avoiding the writing of checks for your home mortgage, utilities, and other bills. In addition, it saves you the trip to the post office, which can be as long as thirty minutes. You also save on the cost of gas and stamps. Online bill paying also prevents you from paying penalties in case you forget to pay bills on time. Ensure that your bank account has at least 1.30 times your total monthly bills when paying online.

A credit card can also be effectively used to save time. Having receipts is different from having a chronological record of your expenses, so you can use a credit card to have a record of your expenses. It provides an independent mechanism to quickly countercheck your receipts. One missed bill payment can make a big difference on your taxes because you won't have an accurate record of your expenditures. Besides, the record provides another means of convincing tax authorities about your business transactions. Pay the credit card bill as soon as possible to ensure you do not incur charges.

8.4 Web Sites Again

No Web site is ever finished. As time goes by, you may add or delete some features on your site. As an example, if you change your telephone number, develop new product or capability, or simply add a white paper, your Web site must change. That is why it pays to spend some time learning the Web site design software used to create your site.

If your business becomes so large that it takes more than one person to maintain the site, it is best to hire an employee to maintain the site. You must provide the specifications on how it should be maintained. In addition, you should always keep a backup copy of all the files, images, and the elements and structure of its navigation. The backup copy provides protection in case the webmaster decides to leave.

8.5 Managing E-mails

You will have tons of e-mails in your business. Since the development of digital technology, tremendous amounts of information flow in and out of a business. Nowadays, anybody can easily draft a presentation file, or any point paper, and send it by e-mail to other employees. Word processing amplified such a capability to a magnitude not historically seen before. As a result, employees spend a significant amount of their time opening, replying, and storing e-mails. It is conceivable that the trend will continue in the future. Therefore, a system of safeguarding your e-mails and minimizing time spent on processing them is in order.

To ensure the privacy of your contacts, use the e-mail feature of your Web site. Do not use the e-mail system of search engines or network providers. They are designed for personal e-mails only.

A business usually has one general e-mail address. For example, the common address is info@myBusiness.com. All incoming e-mails must then be sorted out to different accounts of your business. For example, if you have e-mails for several employees or functions of your business, then an outside e-mail must go to one of the employees or functions. Hence, you must create one or more e-mail accounts or boxes in your system. Again, managing an e-mail system depends on the Web site software.

Another way to save time with e-mails is to learn how to write in a professional, courteous, and quick way. Whether an e-mail is relevant or not, you may have to respond to it. The best way to respond is by replying as soon as you receive it. Quick response requires the ability to write well quickly, which requires quick organization of your thoughts. Effective writing skill is hard to acquire, and practice is the only solution. Therefore, try to write as much as possible.

<u>Business Security</u>. The Internet provides higher efficiency in marketing. It can also be efficient in stealing personal customer information. Ethics require that any customer information be kept private as much as possible.

Use a computer that is not connected to the Internet to record customer information. Any e-mail that you received from any of your customers or business partners must be regarded as confidential. If there is no reason to keep a copy of an e-mail or document, the best thing to do is delete them as quickly as possible. By doing so, a virus has less chance of accessing them.

8.6 Filing System

Businesses nowadays are also buried in a sea of files. Files include extensions such as.doc,.txt,.ppt,.pdf,.html, and so on. It is common for an employee to have hundreds of files in his folders on one or more drives.

The fundamental problem of storing files is to be able to retrieve one as quickly as possible. A file may have different versions.

A sorting algorithm organizes files in a computer usually in ascending order. Files that start with numeric characters have the highest precedence. Next are the files with alphabetic characters. If two file names have a mixture of numeric and alphabetic characters, they will be arranged with the same rules. Note that files are not arranged according to their file extensions. That is, a folder or a drive may have a random pattern of groups of.doc,.txt, or.ppt files.

To illustrate the above, the following files are sorted in a folder:

1xyz.doc
2xyz.txt
3abc.doc
4pqr.ppt

The files are related together in the sense that some of them are revisions or expansions of other files.

Consider renaming the original files as follows:

xyz.doc
xyz.txt
abc.doc
pqr.ppt

Now the files will be sorted and stored as follows:

abc.doc
pqr.ppt
xyz.doc
xyz.txt

Note the changes in the pattern. For example, the original has 1xyz.doc as the first file. In contrast, abc.doc is the first file of the renamed files. In both cases, the sequence of the files is mixed relative to file extensions.

Consider that a folder has hundreds of files with different file extensions. A person who attempts to retrieve a file must first know its extension. Next, she scans all the files with that extension. If she can not find it, she uses the Find feature of an operating system to find the file. Using the feature requires knowledge of the accurate file name. If the file was created months before, it may not be possible to recollect the accurate name of the file. There is the trouble again.

Oftentimes an employee finds himself working on the same class of documents. To track them all the time, he uses the Minimize button to hide a document. The button shows the file name at the lower horizontal navigation bar. If there are five or more files, the filenames are truncated so that they will fit in the bar. The truncated file names, however, become hard to recognize. If the first ten characters of the file names are identical, then the only way to find the correct file to work on is to restore the files one by one.

The above discussion may be summarized by the following principles.

1. Sorting algorithm is beyond the control of an employee.
2. File names are sorted with numeric character having the highest precedence.
3. Files are not arranged according to their extensions.
4. There must be an accurate recollection of the file names.
5. There must exist a capability to work on simultaneous documents using the minimize button.
6. The final version of a class of documents must somehow be flagged.

The above principles must satisfy any convention for naming files. An example of such a convention is as follows:

wn_word1Word2

where,

w = the first character of word1
n = numeric character representing the version number
_ = underscore character
word1 = first descriptor of the file in lower case
Word2 = second descriptor of the file (first character in upper case)

The following are examples of the convention:

1. p1_proposalABC.doc
2. p2_proposalABC.ppt
3. p4_proposalABC.txt
4. p9_proposalABC.pdf

An operating system will, usually, sort the above files first by the letter *p* followed by the numbers 1, 2, 4, and 9. Since they have the same word1 (proposal) and Word2 (ABC), the sorting algorithm will not relocate the file. The different file extensions will have no impact, either, because the first two characters (such as p1) determine the result. The naming convention helps the sorting algorithm by minimizing the number of comparisons of characters. It makes the computer run faster.

Consider a counter example such as a file name p1_privateMemo.doc. The file name p1_privateMemo.doc will appear before p1_proposalABC.doc since the third character, *i,* in *private* has higher precedence than the third character, *o,* in *proposal.*

The filename p2_privateMemo.doc, however, will be inserted between p1_proposalABC.doc and p2_proposalABC.doc. It will create some disorganization. Its probability, however, is small. The proof is as follows.

Since there are twenty-six characters in the alphabet, and there are ten numeric characters, the probability that two file names will have the same first two characters is $(1/26)(1/10) = 1/260$ or slightly more than 0.38%. The probability is small enough to adopt the convention.

8.7 Meetings

People in an organization hold meetings to discuss issues. Sometimes, the same group of people will discuss the same issue repeatedly with no end in sight. This is especially true in ineffective organizations run by incompetent people.

Consider a tank of water. An input or incoming pipe feeds water into the tank. The water leaves the tank from an outgoing pipe. Assume that the water is an issue. If the diameter of the incoming pipe is greater than the diameter of the outgoing pipe, issues will accumulate in the tank. The rate of rise of issues can be described by a first-order differential equation whose general solution is in exponential form. It is given by:

$$I(t) = I_0 e^{kt}$$

where,

I(t) = number of issues at any time t
I_0 = initial number of issues
k = a constant that depends on the diameters of the pipes

Essentially, if the constant k is positive, then issues will accumulate in the tank. Else, if it is negative, then an issue could not accumulate in the tank. That is, the organization can resolve issues as they emerge. The constant k reflects the competence of the people in the meetings.

If k is negative, you have only two choices. The first is to continue membership in the organization. In this choice, you voice your solution to an issue and try to influence the group to adopt your proposed solution. An organization exists to market a product or service. It is a marketing medium. Choosing to stay may give you advantages that may not be evident now but may be evident later.

The second choice is to distance your self from the organization and take the least active part. You may take membership in another organization, which has better leadership. That is, you simply choose an organization whose constant, k, is larger.

8.8 Record Keeping of Home Bills and Other Home Activities

Home bills and transactions with other companies take a significant amount of time from your business. You have to be systematic in recording data on those bills and transactions. Use a notebook to record all transactions that are related to your home. Enter in the notebook essential information, such as the name of the company, date of letter, address of organization, person to contact, amount involved, and summary of the transaction. The notebook is simply a journal of activities related to your home. Do not write sentences for data. Simply write the data. An example is shown below:

1) Company XYZ = 22 May 06, 123 X Street, City Y, State X 92189, point of contact Joe S. Smith, telephone (900) 354-9876, bill for $100, reminder for unpaid bill.

The pattern of the data is simple enough to recollect what each piece of information is about. Writing a sentence for each piece of information will simply take too much time. The idea is to write the essential information only sacrificing structure.

Appendix A

Sample Business Plan and Presentation Slides for TestCubic

The Vision of TestCubic

Provide three-dimensional imaging of test signals.

The Mission

Our mission is to provide the government, defense companies, and manufacturing and testing companies a simple but effective platform to isolate faults due to design, manufacturing, workmanship, or logistics. TestCubic believes the existing point-to-point probing, to isolate faults, is too simple and expensive for today's complex technologies. The company plans to replace such a point-to-point probing with a three-dimensional imaging. Three-dimensional imaging uses two coordinates for position and one coordinate for power. The three coordinates provide sufficient information to accurately locate the component causing failure.

The initial marketing of the products and services will be massive. It will target all the customers described above in addition to the medical industry, which may also find the product useful.

The initial products consist of an array of sensors and amplifiers, a computer, and software to process signals. Services that go with the products include technical support and training.

The manufacture and integration of electronic systems require design, assembly, and test operations. Test operations find faults in design or assembly. Ineffective test operations are usually performed by trial and error and create large a time delay in completing and selling a system. Delay in selling the system implies delay in revenue. In addition, pervasive faults may necessitate redesign or complete cancellation of the system.

Present test technologies also rely on huge expenditures of instruments for stimulus and response. Engineers usually develop test software to apply stimulus and to measure the product's response. Weeks, if not months, are used developing test software. TestCubic will minimize the number of instruments and software by eliminating, as much as possible, instruments designed to measure response. This is possible because the products of TestCubic are by themselves instruments that can measure response. In addition, TestCubic can develop software that can automate test software and minimize test-software development.

There is no alternative but to develop effective test systems such as the one envisioned by TestCubic. By providing a more systematic method to isolate electronic faults, the time to market electronic systems will be shortened dramatically.

Considering that the products of TestCubic will require fewer parts and less software, its comparative advantage over the existing technologies is about five times. This figure is certainly possible because of the three coordinates in three-dimensional imaging. Therefore, if a company invests in test equipment that breaks even in six years, the products of TestCubic will break even in less than two years. A break-even point of two years is excellent.

The Market

A huge portion of the Department of Defense's budget is allocated to operations and maintenance, including maintaining old systems and manufacturing new systems. The test component of operations and maintenance is about 25% of that budget. Given that the Department of Defense gets $400 billion a year, the initial market size of the products is about $100 billion. An advantage of the Department of Defense as a market is that they always have the money.

Manufacturing and test companies also require operations and maintenance. Using a conservative estimate, the initial market size of TestCubic in these companies will probably run to about $100 billion also.

As mentioned before, TestCubic will develop products for the medical industry. TestCubic will address the needs of the medical community to monitor diseases such as sudden infant death syndrome (SIDS).

In the last twenty years, systems have increased in complexity, partly due to digital technology. A single wire carrying an analog signal is now equivalent to ten digital signals. As the number of bits in digital applications increases, the complexity of systems increases. This trend will continue in the near future. Hence, the demand for the products of TestCubic should increase.

TestCubic believes in continuous innovations to match customers' needs. To this end, the company plans to spend a significant part of its revenue on research and development as one of the ways for the company to add value to its products and services.

TestCubic recognizes that marketing is probably one of the most difficult parts of a business operation. For this purpose, TestCubic is now negotiating with some local companies to market its products in the future. These companies are seasoned professionals and have proven records.

The Competition

While there are many manufacturers of test instruments and equipment, none of them manufactures a system that can model test results in three-dimensional form. Two of these companies are Company X and Company Y. TestCubic, however, will use some of instruments, such as switching matrices and amplifiers, from these companies. It will not, however, use instruments such as impedance meters, oscilloscopes, or spectrum analyzers.

The single most important hurdle to overcome in the deployment of the products of TestCubic is to convince its customers of the advantages of three-dimensional imaging of tests. Oftentimes, a new idea takes a long time to take over the old. TestCubic is aware of the possible rejection of its products, especially in its initial marketing.

Product Development

The development of products will consist of three stages. First, products for the defense industry will be developed. Next will be the products for measuring electromagnetic fields for electromagnetic field compliance. Finally, products addressing the needs of the medical community will be developed.

Each product will require application software. Software will be developed in synchronism with the product.

Pricing, Sales, and Revenues

Products of TestCubic can deliver several benefits. These include delaying in production (and revenues) minimally, verifying the design, and characterizing test patterns.

Existing systems are prone to false failures and are unreliable in root cause analysis of test failures. Tedious and time-consuming probing is required to isolate a fault. As an example, a fault in the DC power supply of an electronic card assembly requires probing all the nodes connected to that power supply. If the supply has N nodes, there will be a series of N measurements. Three-dimensional imaging, however, can accomplish all the N measurements in one shot. On the average, the proposed three-dimensional imaging of test results is about five times more efficient than the present conventional systems.

The components of a three-dimensional imaging product are its array of sensors, an amplifier, an analog-to-digital converter, and a portable laptop computer. Results of the analog-to-digital conversion will be stored in a computer buffer. Proprietary software will process data from the memory buffer. Customers will be paying for these components in addition to direct labor, indirect labor, overhead, management costs, and about 30% net profit.

The package of sensors, amplifiers, analog-to-digital converter, and software will initially be priced at about $8,000.00. This is not much compared to automated test equipment costing several hundred thousands of dollars. As an example, test equipment consisting of several bays of power sources and instruments can readily cost $2 million. The $8,000 price will provide enough income to offset the costs of rebates and returns. Field service to support the product will be priced at prevailing labor rates plus management fees. Figure A.1 shows the relationship between price and customer-perceived benefits.

The chief technology officer of this company has been in the engineering business for almost twenty-five years and is fully qualified to develop the hardware and the software for this product. In addition, he had several years of experience in the federal acquisition process. The principal can also develop measures to reduce the costs of goods and services.

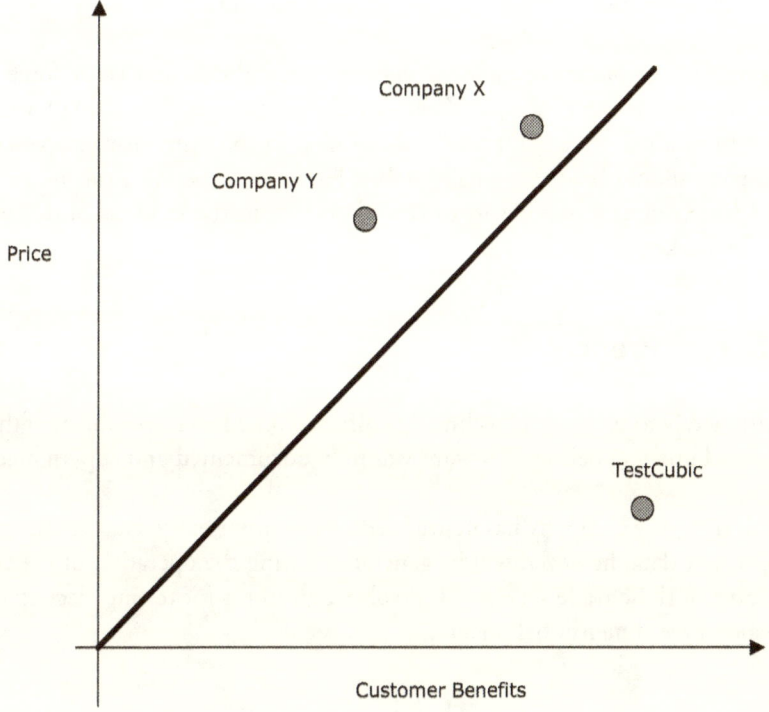

Figure A.1 Price versus Customer Benefits

Break-Even Analysis, Capital Management, Human Resources, and Financial Model

The chief technology officer has spent almost a year of labor in proving the design. In the first six months, TestCubic will incur about $500,000 debt. The debt stems from the management personnel and technicians' wages, material costs for the development of the first prototypes and their improvements, and marketing. Improvements in the prototypes will include factors such as ease of setup and use and ease of interpreting test data. Unknown variables for marketing the product using the Internet, direct sales to customers, patent searches, and participation in trade shows will also be investigated during the first six months.

From six months to one year, TestCubic will be in a production cycle and ready to deliver to its customers. The company will again be in debt for this period. Expected debt is about $500,000 for ten production units.

Expansion of the company's facilities, logistics capabilities, and labor force will start in the second year of operation. A debt of another $4,000,000 will be incurred to produce about 100 production units. In the third year of operation, the company should be operationally stable. However, depending on the market demand, the company may resort to IPO financing in the millions of dollars to match the market.

Intellectual Property

As mentioned before, the chief technology officer worked on the problem of three-dimensional imaging before. His work was fully documented and copyrighted.

As of this time, the company has no trade secrets or proprietary data. Trade secrets or proprietary data, however, will be generated during the operation of the company. Some of these trade secrets will involve algorithms for testing electrical circuits using three-dimensional imaging.

The Ultimate Opportunity—Will the Journey Be Worth It?

In three years, the market value of TestCubic will be around $45,000,000. The bases of the estimate are: (1) increased intellectual properties of the company, (2) firm foothold on the market, and (3) stable management.

The above variables may also be the reason why test companies such as Company X and Company Y may buy the company. That is, the efficiencies of TestCubic products, market positioning, and effective management structure may pose competition with these companies. To minimize that risk, the acquisition of the company may be their best option.

In addition to the above financial gains, there are other benefits for pursuing the vision of TestCubic. Not only does TestCubic address the issue of minimizing costs from operations and maintenance, but it will also address two other vital issues. They are the development of sensors and the synthesis of new algorithms for testing electronic systems. These two areas are so important not only in military applications but in commercial applications, as well. By addressing these fundamental issues, the government and the industry can free dollars from operations and maintenance that can instead be used in basic research. After all, the author believes that basic research is the prime driver of any economy.

Slides

If an entrepreneur is planning to seek money from investors, such as a venture capitalist, he must also prepare slides in addition to the business plan. The slides highlight the main points of the business plan. Prior to making any presentation, ensure that information in the business plan and the slides matches.

The following pages show an example of slides that were derived from the previous business plan.

 # TestCubic

Imaging Test in Three Dimensions

The Vision of TestCubic

- Provide test results of electronic circuits by capturing the three- dimensional image of its test signals.

- Presenter: Usually the chief technology officer and the chief executive officer.

TestCubic

Imaging Test in Three Dimensions

Functions of TestCubic

- TestCubic develops test equipment for electronics manufacturers and defense industry companies.

- TestCubic simplifies the problem of finding the root cause of software or electronic failures.

- TestCubic is a three-dimensional imaging product. Existing technologies use laborious, time-consuming, point-to-point probing of contacts to find failures in electronic circuits.

TestCubic

Imaging Test in Three Dimensions

Relieving the Pain

- TestCubic simplifies test operations by providing two coordinates for position and one coordinate for electrical power. TestCubic is at least nine times more efficient than existing systems.

- The principal has been in the testing business for about fifteen years. During that time, the complexity of electronic systems has increased exponentially. In addition, lots of overhead labor is spent trying to find out the root cause of failures.

- Compared to investment in existing systems, TestCubic's return on investment will be nine times more than investment in existing systems. Comparatively, a company that invests in TestCubic will break even in one year as opposed to nine years for a company investing in existing systems.

- TestCubic equipment is a highly specialized system. Users must know the signature of a good electronic system as the reference in testing production units. This high degree of specialization implies that TestCubic could not become a commodity.

TestCubic

Imaging Test in Three Dimensions

The Market and Its Customers

- The two biggest markets for TestCubic are the defense industry and electronics manufacturing companies. The defense industry alone is about a $400 billion market. Commercial manufacturers of TVs, radios, computers, telecommunications equipment, medical instrumentation, security devices, and industrial control electronics have the market size of approximately $1 trillion.

- TestCubic will target all companies that manufacture or troubleshoot the basic building blocks of electronic systems. TestCubic is expected to grow exponentially because of the exponential increase in the complexity of systems brought by digital technologies.

TestCubic

Imaging Test in Three Dimensions

The Management Team

- CEO—your company CEO

- CTO—your chief technology officer

- CMO—your chief marketing manager

- CFO—your chief financial officer

- Identify who of the above will work on the project full-time and part-time

- Board of Directors—provide the list

TestCubic

Imaging Test in Three Dimensions

Competition and Barriers

- At the present, TestCubic has no competition in three-dimensional imaging of test results. The best companies in the United States still use point-to-point probing. Companies in TestCubic markets will have to adopt its product to be competitive (i.e., 900% more efficient). TestCubic products will require software to automate tests. Software will be written in a programming language that is object-oriented. Existing companies use C, C++, or Basic. Competing companies will have to change their programming language to compete against TestCubic.

- The keys in TestCubic products are its sensors and test algorithm. TestCubic is also investigating new sensors and developing algorithms.

- TestCubic will always maintain a lead in competition by hiring innovative employees. When fully organized, it will maintain links with the education community, test engineering community, and the government. It will also subsidize graduate students' research.

TestCubic

Imaging Test in Three Dimensions

Marketing, Sales, and Support

- TestCubic will use the following media to market its product: Web site, trade shows, newspapers, and, of course, word of mouth. It will also send letters to government agencies announcing the TestCubic product. Its Web site will be populated with how-to instructions on using the product. In addition, the site will have a query form for customer questions, secure transactions, and so on. The company will do all the marketing, sales, and support.

- There will be no indirect channel.

TestCubic

Imaging Test in Three Dimensions

Expected Growth Pattern

- Sensors and test algorithms will be investigated and developed during the first three months of the business. Next, a prototype will be made. The prototype will include not only sensors but also other electronics and computer system. Ten units of the production version will be produced starting the seventh month. From the first to the last day of the second year, the organization must have the capability to produce at least ten units a month.

- TestCubic will be operational and organized at the beginning of its third year. All the technical, marketing, and organizational requirements of the business will be solved in its first two years of operation. Around the fourth or fifth year, the business could be ready for acquisition or initial public offering.

- The principal of TestCubic proved the underlying concept of the product in his master's thesis. He sees no major risk. TestCubic's product can be easily adapted to applications such as medical imaging and non-test applications.

TestCubic

Imaging Test in Three Dimensions

Table A.1 Sample Form for Expected Financial Growth

	Last 12 Mo.	This Year	Mo. 13-24	Mo. 25-36	Mo. 37-48
New Customers					
Units Shipped					
Revenues					
Gross Profit					
Gross Margin %					
SG&A					
EBITDA					
Cashflow					
Cum. Cashflow					

- TestCubic may experience sudden and universal acceptance of its product. In this case, the company will have to expand. Training of employees in the assembly and integration of the product is minimal. Therefore, expansion could be easily implemented.

- It is also possible for TestCubic to experience negative cash flow. This is the reason why innovators of TestCubic must line up new products down the line. That is, the company will research and develop new applications and markets.

TestCubic

Imaging Test in Three Dimensions

Table A.2 Sample Form of Valuation and Dilution Analysis

Round No.	Premoney valuation ($Million)	Amount to raise ($Million)	Postmoney valuation ($Million)	Total (%)	Share of Founders (% and $Million)	Round 1 investors (% and $Million)	Round 2 investors (% and $Million)	IPO investors (% and $Million)
1	$1M	$1M	$2M	100	63%	37%		
					$1.26M	$0.74M		
2	$4M	$2M	$6M	100	39%	23%	38%	
					$2.34M	$1.38M	$2.28M	
IPO	$45M	$15M	$60M	100	24%	14%	24%	37%
					$14.4M	$8.4M	$14.4M	$22.2M

Notes:
1. More than two rounds may be required.
2. The premoney valuation is the perceived value in terms of intellectual properties, market penetration, expertise in the industry, existing organization, and other factors.
3. Describe the uses of each amount raised for each round and IPO.
4. Note that as the number of rounds increases, the founders' percentage decreases because most of the shares go to investors.

 # TestCubic

Imaging Test in Three Dimensions

Acquisition and Additional Value

- TestCubic will not be acquired in the first two years of operation. The investment community will take time to digest the capabilities and potential of TestCubic. However, in three to five years the company may be acquired. Possible companies might be one of the defense companies. Defense companies are heavily involved in tests. Acquiring TestCubic may reduce their cost of operations. Test and measurement companies may also acquire TestCubic. While TestCubic does not directly compete against test and measurement companies, production of TestCubic offers an unprecedented scale in efficiency (nine times or 900%).

- The most difficult parts of TestCubic's technology are its sensors and test algorithms. They are the major intellectual properties of the company. Future work on these parts may yield applications that are beyond its initial application. Success in enhancing these parts can contribute as much as 200% to the value of the company.

TestCubic

Imaging Test in Three Dimensions

Risks

- TestCubic will develop assembly and test instructions to ensure the quality of its product. No in-house manufacturing is anticipated at this time. Manufacturing will only be performed if sensors are no longer commercially available.

- The TestCubic product will consist of sensors, switching matrix, amplifiers, analog-to-digital converter, and computer. The principal of TestCubic developed generic specifications to ensure the quality of the parts.

- Ideally, the TestCubic product must use a sensor that has the widest bandwidth. Larger bandwidth minimizes the need for extra sensors. While such a sensor may not exist in the market, its lack of availability does not pose a risk in realizing TestCubic's product.

- TestCubic's product is a simple integration of the above parts. Personnel will be trained professionally in the integration of the parts to ensure their job satisfaction and retention.

- TestCubic will minimize expenses to preserve capital and maximize investor's return.

Appendix B

Generic Requirements for a Web Site

<u>Name</u>. The name of the Web site shall be HardwareParts.

<u>Contact for revenues</u>. The Web site shall contain the address of a bank, which holds the account of HardwareParts. Buyers of the parts will route their funds to the bank via secure Internet payment service.

<u>Contact for technical and customer service assistance</u>. Use a telephone answering service to provide a twenty-four-hour service for questions. Contract with the telephone answering service shall be with HardwareParts.

<u>Preamble for the site</u>. The preamble for the site describes the product, the value a customer can get from it, and the support she can expect. It must be enticing and compelling.

<u>Graphics</u>. Provide graphics, such as pictures of parts, in JPEG format.

<u>Support statement</u>. Provide a statement showing that if a customer is not satisfied, a full refund will be provided (less shipping costs). Solicit feedback for future use.

<u>Use of search words</u>. Compile a list of at least ten search words. Test the search words by actually using them in an Internet search engine. Make a listing of sites for each search word and determine competing sites. Use the search words of the competing sites.

<u>Fonts</u>. Fonts shall be as follows:

1. Header of headers (main topic or chapter): Arial, bold, number 13.5 to 14
2. Header of a paragraph (subtopic): Arial, bold, number 12
3. Body of paragraphs: Verdana, non-bold, number 10

The spacing between the main topic, subtopics, and paragraphs shall be as follows:

Main Topic (or Chapter) (Arial, bold, size 14)
One Space with size 14 bold Arial

Subtopic 1 (Arial, bold size 12)
-single space between subtopic and paragraph (Verdana, non-bold, size 10)
Paragraph 1 (Verdana, non-bold, size 10)
-single space between paragraphs (Verdana, non-bold, size 10)
Paragraph 2 (Verdana, non-bold, size 10)

Double space between last paragraph and next subtopic (Verdana, non-bold, size 10)

Subtopic 2 (Arial, bold size 12)

<u>Maximum length of a paragraph</u>. All paragraphs shall be no more than length of an eyeglass frame. The number of words in a line of a paragraph should be around ten to eleven words.

<u>Search engine optimization</u>. The Web site shall follow the design, technical, and quality guidelines as shown in industry standards. Some of these guidelines are summarized in the following paragraphs.

For the design guidelines, observe the following:

1. Do not use dynamic pages.

2. Use clear, useful, and accurate information.
3. Links should be text, rather than graphics.
4. Each page in the site should be accessible from at least one or more links.
5. The site contains the search words.

The following are the technical guidelines:

1. Use commercially available software to test the site.
2. Do not use session IDs to access the site.
3. Ensure that the server supports the search requirements of the most widely used search engines.
4. Use robots.txt file to permit search engines to "crawl" your site.
5. The site map should be submitted to other search engines.

The If-Modified-Since-HTTP header tells a search engine if the content of the site has changed since last visited by its crawler. See http://www.robotstxt.org/wc/faq.html for information on how to generate the robots.txt file.

Some of the quality guidelines are shown below:

1. Put the emphasis on users, not on the search engines.
2. Don't deliberately try tricks to improve rankings.
3. Avoid linking to sites of web spammers.
4. Use authorized programs to monitor the visitor statistics.
5. The site has no virus or Trojans.

For the first item, design the Web site as if there is no search engine. Do not use tricks or schemes, such as the use of doorway pages or sneaky redirects, to improve the ranking of the site. Contact the search engine provider to find authorized programs that monitor visitor statistics.

Proposed layout. Lay out the main page such that it is balanced, practical, and capable of expanding with minimum changes. Figure B.1 shows the outline of the proposed layout.

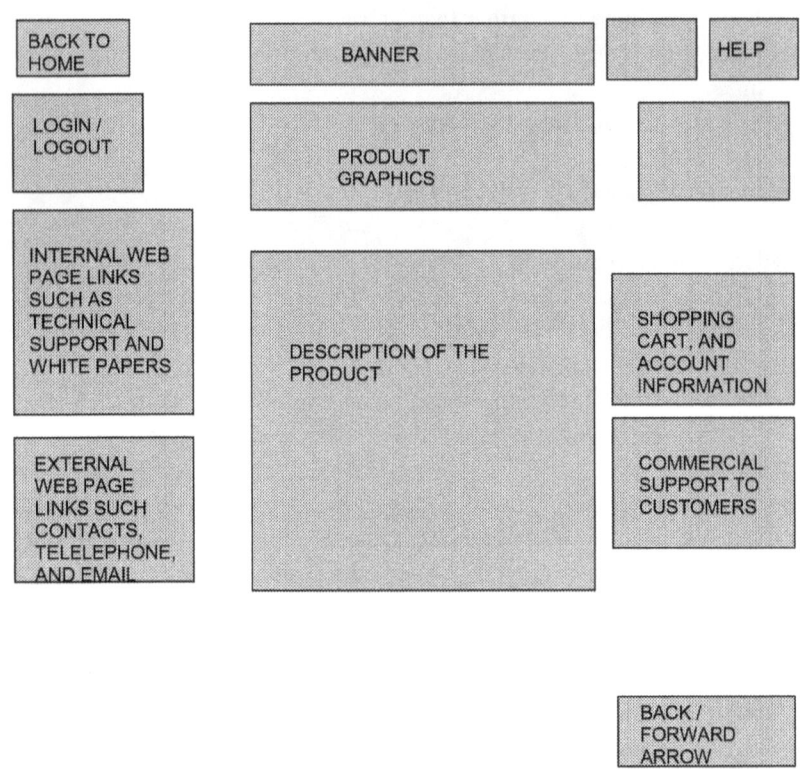

Figure B.1 Layout of Common Elements in a Web Site

References

1. Goodman, Joseph W., *Introduction to Fourier Optics*. Roberts & Company Publishers, 2005.

2. Beyer, William H., *CRC Standard Mathematical Tables*. Florida: CRC Press, 1978.

3. Anthony, R. and Pearlman, L., *Essentials of Accounting*. Addison-Wesley, 2000.

4. Constance, John D., *Electrical Engineering for Professional Engineering Examination*. McGraw-Hill. 1984.

5. An excellent source for designing websites may be found in *www.google.com/support/webmasters/*.

About the Author

Jesus C. de Sosa has bachelor's degree and a master's degree in electrical engineering from San Diego State University. In addition, he has bachelor's degree in mathematics from Adamson University, Philippines. He was an adjunct professor of mathematics at San Diego City College and held various electrical engineering positions with the government, the construction industry, and the defense industry.

In early 2006, he encountered the problem of renting out a new house he bought a year earlier. His neighborhood had four competing homes for rent. Competition was stiff. The popular belief then was to minimize improvement in a house if it was to be for rent. He abandoned the belief. Instead, he maximized the improvements and provided inducement to the renter to take care of the house. In the end, his house was the first to be rented. Starting from this simple experience, he further investigated the elements of a new business start-up. This book encapsulates the elements he discovered. Jesus C. de Sosa is also the author of the book, "Discoveries in Black Jack: Strategies and Mathematics".

978-0-595-40262-5
0-595-40262-3